SENEGAL
in Pictures

VGS

Tom Streissguth

Twenty-First Century Books

Contents

Lerner Publishing Group, Inc., realizes that current information and statistics quickly become out of date. To extend the usefulness of the Visual Geography Series, we developed www.vgsbooks.com, a website offering links to up-to-date information, as well as in-depth material, on a wide variety of subjects. All the websites listed on www.vgsbooks.com have been carefully selected by researchers at Lerner Publishing Group, Inc. However, Lerner Publishing Group, Inc., is not responsible for the accuracy or suitability of the material on any website other than www.lernerbooks.com. It is recommended that students using the Internet be supervised by a parent or teacher. Links on www.vgsbooks.com will be regularly reviewed and updated as needed.

Website address: www.lernerbooks.c

Twenty-First Century Books
A division of Lerner Publishing Group, Inc.
241 First Avenue North
Minneapolis, MN 55401 U.S.A.

web enhanced @ www.vgsbooks.com

CULTURAL LIFE   46

► Music and Dance. Literature. Arts and Crafts. Sports and Recreation. Food. Holidays and Festivals.

THE ECONOMY   56

► Services. Manufacturing, Mining and Energy. Agriculture and Fishing. Transportation. Media and Communications. The Future.

FOR MORE INFORMATION

Library of Congress Cataloging-in-Publication Data

Streissguth, Thomas, 1958–
    Senegal in pictures / by Tom Streissguth.
      p.   cm. — (Visual geography series)
    Includes bibliographical references and index.
    ISBN 978-1-57505-951-8 (lib. bdg. : alk. paper)
    1. Senegal—Juvenile literature. I. Title.
DT549.22.S77 2009
966.3—dc22   2008024703

Manufactured in the United States of America
1 2 3 4 5 6 – BP – 14 13 12 11 10 09

INTRODUCTION

On the western bulge of Africa lies the Republic of Senegal. African and European traditions mark this nation of 12.8 million people. Senegal was a colony of France for a century. The country won its independence in 1960. Since that time, it has remained a democratic nation. It has also built a strong modern economy.

People have lived in the area of Senegal for thousands of years. Starting in the fourth century A.D., mighty African empires based outside Senegal ruled the east. Local kingdoms, including the Wolof kingdom, arose in other parts of Senegal. In the tenth century A.D., Senegal began to trade regularly with North Africa. This contact brought the religion of Islam to the region. Christianity came with the first Europeans in the mid-fifteenth century. Europeans built trading posts on Senegal's Atlantic coast. They also settled the valley of the Senegal River.

The Portuguese, Dutch, and British sought workers for plantations (large farms) in the Americas. Slave traders expanded western African slavery into a big business. They captured people from the interior

and brought them to coastal trading stations. Traders then put the captives aboard ships for the voyage across the Atlantic Ocean. The Guinea coast—from Senegal south to the mouth of the Congo River in central Africa—was the center of this trade. Slave depots in Senegal held thousands of captives at a time. The slave trade flourished until the European nations banned it in the nineteenth century.

In the late eighteenth century, the French colonized most of western Africa. They made the port city of Dakar, Senegal, their headquarters. After World War II (1939–1945), many Senegalese (and other Africans under European rule) demanded self-rule. In other parts of the continent, the struggle for independence caused bitter political and military conflict. But Senegal won its independence from France peacefully in 1960. Its first president was Léopold Sédar Senghor. This skilled politician was also a world-famous poet.

Modern Senegal is a land of many faces. The capital, Dakar, is a bustling port city. In the south, farmers cultivate small plots of land.

Children play soccer on a sunny beach near Dakar on a Sunday afternoon.

The sandy beaches of the Atlantic coast draw tourists from around the world. In the west and north, Senegalese herders raise cattle, sheep, and goats. The eastern region struggles with a severe drought. The lack of rain there has forced many farming families to move to cities. Senegal is dealing with poverty, unemployment, and environmental problems. The government also struggles to provide adequate education and health care.

Despite European influences, Senegal is proudly an African nation. French is the official language, but a majority of people speak the Wolof language. Traditional clothing styles and family ties are very much a part of the western African heritage. Senegalese artists and authors freely combine European and African styles. Senegal also maintains close alliances with other nations in Africa.

The Senegalese enjoy a vibrant and democratic society. In recent years, their economy has grown and their standard of living has improved. Despite their many challenges, they are proud of their country and its successes.

Visit www.vgsbooks.com for links to websites with additional information about the land, history, people, culture, and economy of Senegal.

THE LAND

Senegal, on the western tip of Africa, covers an area of about 75,955 square miles (196,722 square kilometers). It is about the size of the state of Nebraska. On the north is Mauritania. Mali lies to the east. Southern Senegal borders Guinea and Guinea-Bissau. The Atlantic Ocean forms the western coast.

The narrow Republic of the Gambia extends like a finger into Senegal for 200 miles (322 km). Gambia begins where the Gambia River meets the ocean. The country nearly cuts off Senegal's southern Casamance region.

◉ Topography

Senegal's topography, or landscape, consists mostly of low, rolling plains. There are five major geographical regions: the coastal zone, the Senegal River valley, the Ferlo, eastern Senegal or the Sahel, and the Casamance.

The coastal zone runs about 310 miles (499 km) along the Atlantic

Ocean. Sandy beaches line the coast. Sandbars offshore make navigation difficult for ships. Near the middle of the coastal zone is the Cap-Vert peninsula. Dakar sprawls across this narrow piece of land, which is touched on three sides by the Atlantic. Toward the north, the coastal belt is about 15 to 20 miles (24 to 32 km) wide. The southern half of the zone is much narrower. Rivers and creeks meet the sea on the coast. Mangrove trees grow on flat, swampy islands off the coast.

The Senegal River floods each year. This allows farming in the Senegal River valley, which runs north and west along the northern border with Mauritania. Most of the valley is about 10 miles (16 km) wide. It broadens to about 35 miles (56 km) where the river reaches the Atlantic.

The people of the valley live and work by the river's yearly flood. In the rainy season, the river overflows its banks. It spreads out until almost the entire valley is underwater. Villages, which rise on higher

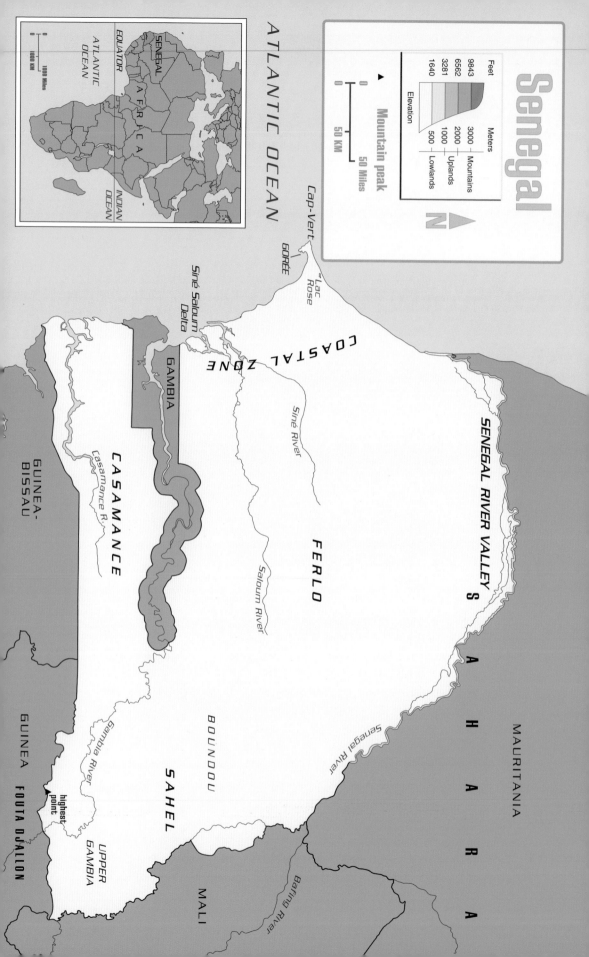

ground, stand out as temporary islands. When the waters recede, farmers sow their crops. After the harvest, the land remains dry until the next seasonal flood.

The broad Ferlo plain covers west central Senegal. Only a small amount of rain falls there every year. The soil absorbs most of the moisture. The sandy soil and poor rainfall make farming difficult. Permanent villages, therefore, are few. Many farmers have moved out of the region to settle on more productive land.

Eastern Senegal is part of the Sahel, a region that crosses Africa south of the Sahara. Within Senegal, the southern half of the Sahel is called Upper Gambia, or the Niokolo. The northern section is the Boundou. The dry climate in the Boundou is like Ferlo's. Farther south, in Upper Gambia, rainfall increases. Vegetation thrives along with abundant wildlife. In the southeast, the terrain rises to 1,640 feet (500 meters), the highest point. These highlands form the foothills of the Fouta Djallon Mountains. The mountains extend into Guinea.

The Casamance in southern Senegal is the rainiest part of the country. Vegetation thrives in Casamance's humid climate, which allows farmers to grow a greater variety of crops than in northern Senegal.

Rivers

Three major rivers drain large areas of Senegal. Their width varies with the amount of rainfall. In the dry season, large boats avoid these waterways. Only the widest portions near the outlets remain open to cargo ships and large fishing boats.

Palm trees grow along the **coast of the Casamance.** The region's beautiful beaches make it popular with tourists.

Children play on the **banks of the Senegal River** in the town of Saint-Louis.

The Senegal River rises in the Fouta Djallon Mountains of Guinea. The river flows northward and westward for about 1,000 miles (1,609 km). It crosses the border with Mali and flows westward through Senegal before emptying into the Atlantic Ocean. The river divides the Sahel region to the north and more fertile regions to the south.

During the dry season, the Senegal's water level falls. Strong ocean tides move inland as far as 300 miles (483 km) upstream. These tidal waters create saltwater swamps. During the rainy season, the water level rises. At this time, large boats can navigate the river between Saint-Louis in northwestern Senegal and Kayes in Mali. The rest of the year, large boats can travel upstream for only 175 miles (282 km). The river town of Podor serves as an important cargo port for nearby Mauritania.

The Gambia River also begins in Guinea. It enters Senegal near the town of Kédougou in the southeast. It flows through the country for about 200 miles (322 km). The river then runs through Gambia before emptying into the Atlantic Ocean.

The Casamance River is about 200 miles (322 km) long. It draws most of its water from streams in the Casamance. The river flows toward the Atlantic, growing to 5 miles (8 km) wide at its estuary (area where a river meets an ocean). The most important seaport in the region, Ziguinchor, lies about 40 miles (64 km) upstream.

The Saloum River runs for 100 miles (161 km) north of the Gambia River. The Saloum holds salt water from the ocean. Ships can navigate about 60 miles (97 km) of the Saloum. But its salty waters are unfit for watering crops.

Climate

Senegal lies in the tropics, the area of the globe near the equator (the half-way point between the North Pole and the South Pole). The tropics are among Earth's hottest regions, where temperatures vary little between summer and winter. In Senegal, temperatures reach highs of 110°F (43°C) during the day and drop as low as 60°F (16°C) at night. Periods of twilight are shorter in the tropics than in the temperate zones. Thus, full daylight and complete darkness arrive quickly rather than gradually.

Senegal experiences two major seasons, dry and rainy. The rainy season—between June and October—has an average rainfall of 10 inches (25 centimeters) in the north. Average annual rainfall measures 25 inches (64 cm) in Dakar and 60 inches (152 cm) in the Casamance region. The dry season—from November to June—is virtually rainless. The rainy season begins in the south when the monsoon, a rain-bearing wind, reaches Senegal from the ocean and then pushes northward across the land. At this time, a hot and dusty wind known as the harmattan blows across the Sahara. In contrast, during the dry months, ocean currents bring cooler temperatures in the coastal zone.

Fauna

Senegal hosts a great diversity of animal species, many of which are endangered. Some inhabit a 430,000-acre (174,014-hectare) game preserve in the southeast, Niokolo-Koba National Park. The park is home to the country's largest concentration of animals—including lions, leopards, hippopotamuses, warthogs, gazelles and other antelope, and savanna monkeys. Pythons and poisonous snakes—such as vipers, cobras, and mambas—thrive in the Casamance region. A small number of crocodiles inhabit the Senegal River and the Upper Gambia.

Among the most plentiful of the fish found off the coast of Senegal is the large Nile perch, or *capitaine*. This fish is an important source of food for the Senegalese. Shores and estuaries are rich

The **patas monkey** lives in the savannas, or grasslands, of Senegal. It is the fastest runner of all monkeys.

with shrimp and many kinds of saltwater fish. Farther out in the Atlantic, tuna, amberjacks, and dolphins are abundant.

Senegal has huge numbers of seabirds—pelicans, herons, egrets, cormorants, and various terns and ducks—that inhabit the estuaries and the seashore. Among the land birds are ostriches, bustards, quails, partridges, and long-legged secretary birds. The forest is the home of hornbills and large groups of noisy parrots. Vultures and kites are common scavengers that favor settled areas. Migratory birds arrive each winter in Senegal from the cold northern climates of Europe.

○ Flora

There are variations throughout Senegal in rainfall and soil conditions. The savanna, which covers northern Senegal except for the coastal zone, is a region of grasslands, acacia trees, desert date trees, and small, thorny bushes. Farmers use some kinds of acacia trees as cattle feed. Other trees provide gum arabic, a sticky substance used in candies and medicines.

Central Senegal has a more varied mixture of grasslands and trees. Many species are useful in food and commercial goods. Trees in this region include mahogany and the shea tree, which yields a vegetable fat called shea butter. The *kinkeliba* tree has medicinal properties that can reduce fevers, such as those brought on by malaria.

Along the coast north of Dakar, vegetation grows abundantly in a humid, rainy zone. Oil palms, fruit trees, and garden vegetables are common. In areas nearer the ocean, however, only salt-resistant plants can thrive. These species include salt cedars, a few varieties of acacia and mimosa trees, and clumps of salt grass.

Heavy rainfall and fertile soil make the western Casamance the

THE NATIONAL TREE

One of the most important trees in Senegal, as well as throughout Africa, is the baobab. The wood of the baobab is too soft and spongy for timber. But the fruit is edible, and the leaves are used in soups. Furthermore, rope makers can use the bark of the tree, which also is useful as a medicine. To keep water fresh and cool, people store it in the large, natural cavities of the baobab trunk. Players of the traditional board game mancala use baobab seeds as counters. The trees also serve as meeting places in many villages. Senegalese politicians gather crowds under the shade of a baobab to make speeches and ask for votes during election campaigns. Many people believe that older baobab trees house spirits and can serve as guides in making important life decisions.

country's most densely forested region. Mangrove thickets line coastal channels and estuaries. Raffia and rattan palms cluster in dense groves. Oil palms, mahogany, and teak grow on higher ground. Farmers have cleared large areas of Casamance for rice paddies (watery plots used for growing rice).

Environmental Issues

Senegal faces a variety of natural and man-made environmental problems. Since the Sahel drought began in the 1970s, northern Senegal has lost much of its fertile farmland to desertification, or the process of land becoming desert. The drought, overgrazing by livestock, and the cutting of trees for fuel and construction material also causes deforestation, or the loss of tree and plant cover, as well as the erosion of soil by wind or water. This robs the soil of nutrients, making farming more difficult and forcing many families off the land altogether. Annual sandstorms cause further damage.

In Dakar and other large cities of Senegal, heavy traffic, poor sanitation, and polluted waterways affect public health. Open drains and contaminated drinking water can cause a variety of diseases. Most urban areas, however, have access to safe water. City dwellers also suffer lung diseases from polluted air. Traffic snarls and factory emissions cause frequent smog in Dakar. In addition, industries have drained their wastes into Senegal's waterways for many years. Polluted runoff

Residents of this village planted hundreds of **trees at the edge of the desert** to keep it from expanding into their farms.

Heavy traffic clogs the streets of Dakar.

and waste affects many miles of coastline, in turn, harming tourism and the fishing industry. In addition, overfishing has depleted the once-abundant stocks of fish found in the coastal waters.

Senegal tries to protect its endangered animals, including the eland and several species of wild turtle. The nation has set aside about 10 percent of its land as national parks and protected areas. This helps stop illegal hunting and new construction that robs wildlife of its natural habitat. The government has also banned mining in these protected areas. Government policy helps mining companies prospect in new, unprotected regions.

Natural Resources

Senegal lacks significant natural resources, but the country does exploit deposits of phosphates, iron ore, gold, copper, peat, uranium, and titanium. Marble, sandstone, and limestone quarries provide construction material. There are small deposits of oil and natural gas. The severe drought affecting northern Senegal has depleted once-fertile farmland. Fish from rivers and the sea have long provided a dependable food resource. The forests of the south are important sources of firewood and timber.

Senegal has had difficulty managing its natural resources. The country has allowed uncontrolled timber cutting, which has brought about soil erosion and a loss of habitat. Hunting has affected animal populations. In recent years, the country has set up several reserves to protect wildlife. It also has set down stricter laws governing mining.

Cities

The cities of Senegal are growing rapidly with the migration of people from the countryside. About 41 percent of the population lives in urban areas. Large shantytowns rise on the outskirts of Dakar and other cities, while overcrowding affects many neighborhoods. In some places, public services such as electricity and a water supply still do not meet the needs of city dwellers.

DAKAR is the capital and largest city of Senegal, with a population of about one million. Rising on the narrow Cap-Vert peninsula, Dakar is the westernmost city in Africa. For more than a century, it has been a leading seaport. A group of small villages, including Ndakarou, existed on the site in the fifteenth century, when the Portuguese settled the offshore island of Gorée. In the mid-nineteenth century, the French founded a military outpost on the site and adapted the name of Ndakarou to Dakar.

In 1887 a French colonial administration began to govern the city. This regime built railroads, roads, port facilities, and telegraph lines. Dakar became the capital of French West Africa in 1902. As a commercial hub, it attracted merchants, trading firms, banks, and manufacturing companies. When Senegal gained independence in 1960, Dakar became the seat of the new government.

Modern Dakar blends new and old architecture. Churches and mosques (Islamic houses of worship) dot the cityscape. The minarets, or tall towers, of the Great Mosque overlook nearby streets. The elaborately tiled courtyards and interiors of these structures draw many visitors. Elsewhere, tall office and apartment buildings line the city's wide avenues. Structures from French colonial days serve as government offices. Cheikh Anta Diop University opened its doors in 1957. The city also hosts museums and the national zoo.

The old Medina quarter houses several thousand people in a jumble of alleys and narrow streets. People from all over Africa crowd the streets. Open-air marketplaces offer everything from Japanese transistor radios to raw honey from the Casamance. Flowers, vegetables, spices, clothing, shoes, and woven goods attract buyers.

The busy port of Dakar can accommodate up to fifty oceangoing vessels at one time. Besides handling cargo, Dakar also provides water, food, and repair services for

AFRICA'S LAST SUNSET

The Cap-Vert ("Green Cape" in French) includes the capital of Dakar and is the westernmost point on the African mainland. It is the last place the light of the setting sun touches on the continent.

ships. Refrigerated warehouses and pipelines for oil and liquid chemicals add to the port's importance.

Gorée, a former slave-trading station, is part of Dakar. This island lies about a mile (1.6 km) from the mainland. Portuguese, Dutch, British, and French traders brought captives from the interior to the coast. Slave traders transported them from the mainland to Gorée in small boats. European merchants then took their captives to the New World for sale to owners of cotton, indigo, sugar, and tobacco plantations.

TOUBA (population 529,000) is the second-largest city in Senegal. Sheikh Amadou Bamba founded the city in 1887 as a home for the Mouridiya sect that he led in opposition to the colonial government. Modern Touba attracts pilgrims from far and wide to the Grand Magal, a religious festival. The city's Great Mosque, completed in 1963, is one of the largest Islamic religious structures in Africa.

THIÈS (population 238,000) is just east of Dakar. It is a major industrial, commercial, and communications city. It lies at the junction of main highways from Dakar to eastern Senegal, allowing it to serve as an important market for peanuts and other crops in the region. The French established a military post at Thiès in 1864 and linked the city to the Dakar-Niger Railway.

The rail industry marked the modern history of Thiès. A major strike, or work stoppage, by railroad workers inspired the post-World War II movement for independence. As Dakar has expanded eastward, Thiès has attracted investment from foreign and domestic companies. A famous tapestry workshop operates in Thiès. The city's factories also package food, consumer goods, and meat.

RUFISQUE (population 284,000) is an industrial town that has grown rapidly into a suburb of nearby Dakar. Rufisque supports peanut-oil refineries, a pharmaceutical plant, and textile and shoe factories.

KAOLACK (population 172,000) is the capital of the Kaolack region. It serves as the hub of the richest peanut-growing area in Senegal. Kaolack has grown from a small village into a major city. A port for vessels sailing the Saloum River, Kaolack also lies at the end of a branch of the Dakar-Niger Railway. A highway crosses Gambia and links the city with the Casamance district.

After the ban on slavery in the 1800s, the French colonial authorities developed peanut raising. Peanut processing and salt mining are the two busiest industries in modern Kaolack. The city is also home to the Tijaniyah, a religious order that has lodges (branch houses) in several

Farmers sell fruit and vegetables in the streets of Saint-Louis.

other countries. The Medina Bay Mosque, in the center of town, is one of Senegal's most important religious monuments.

SAINT-LOUIS (population 154,000), situated at the mouth of the Senegal River, was once the capital. It also served Senegal as an important seaport. After the railway line between Dakar and Saint-Louis allowed trade to pass more efficiently from the interior through the larger and modern port of Dakar, however, the city lost its place as a major commercial seaport. Nevertheless, it remains the end point for traffic on the Senegal River. Saint-Louis also serves as the gateway to Mauritania, Senegal's neighbor just north of the city.

ZIGUINCHOR (population 70,000) is the main city of the Casamance region and was founded by the Portuguese in 1645. It provides a seaport for the farms, fisheries, sawmills, and peanut-oil complexes in the south. Ziguinchor is one of the country's fastest-growing cities. The city offers regular air service to Dakar, as well as to Conakry in Guinea.

Visit www.vgsbooks.com for links to websites with additional information about Senegal's natural resources. Find out more about visiting the country's national parks and cities.

HISTORY AND GOVERNMENT

Numerous stone monuments and burial sites show that humans have lived for many thousands of years in Senegal. In prehistoric times, however, the climate was very different. The Sahara lay to the north and east. The land of Senegal in this era was more fertile. Gradually, under the press of a changing climate, the desert moved southward. The east and north became dry grassland. This terrain was better for raising livestock than crops. Settlement patterns changed, with herding groups separating themselves from settled farmers.

Archaeologists have found rock wall paintings, iron and stone tools, and pottery in the Senegal River valley. These remains suggest that a large-scale village—or even a city—existed in this area at least 2,500 years ago. These villages traded with other production centers in western Africa. Goods moved along the rivers and up and down the coast. Over time, the control of trade and metalworking passed to a wealthy aristocracy. Villages organized around a chief and his clan. The first small kingdoms arose. These small states vied for trade and territory.

As early as the third century B.C., the inhabitants of central Senegal began raising groups of stone circles near the Gambia River. These circles, which number in the hundreds, are made of tall rock pillars. They mark important burial sites and mounds. Stonecutters skillfully cut and shaped the pillars with iron tools. The stone pillars and circles show that a hardy and well-organized society must have existed in Senegal well before recorded history.

A people known as the Takrur settled the Senegal River valley in the first centuries A.D. The Takrur eventually formed a powerful kingdom. They controlled trade in gold, salt, and slaves. These goods arrived from distant points in the Sahara and to the south, in the Niger River valley.

In the meantime, the kingdom of Namandirou grew on the upper Senegal River. Led by family dynasties known as lineages, the Namandirou paid tribute, or taxes, to the kingdom of Ghana. (This empire is not the same as the modern nation of Ghana.) The Ghana

A SHELL ISLAND OF THE DEAD

Dioran Boumak, an island on the Saloum River, is an artificial island made completely of shells. Historians date the island to the eighth century A.D. Over the centuries, local people used it as a dump for shells, broken pottery, and other items. The island measures 1,300 feet (396 m) long and contains more than one hundred burial sites.

Fadiouth Island is one of Senegal's artificial shell islands. It has been used as a cemetery for centuries.

kings grew wealthy from the trade in gold and became the main rival of the smaller realms in Senegal.

Several other early empires rose east of Senegal. These realms traded in slaves, gold, salt, and spices. Goods traveled by caravan northward and eastward through the Sahara. To control and safeguard these trade routes, the western African states raised strong armies and gradually extended their influence over larger and larger areas.

◐ Conversion to Islam

The first written sources that mention Senegal are chronicles in the Arabic language. Arab traders who came across the Sahara from North Africa kept these records, the earliest of which date to the tenth century A.D. The chronicles show that ancestors of modern Pular-speaking, Serer, and Wolof populations emigrated from lands to the north and east. They moved into the Senegal River valley and other parts of the country.

From the tenth century, the people of Senegal had constant contact with North Africa. Trading caravans came regularly to exchange goods.

North African traders converted the local people to the Islamic religion. (This religion had arisen on the Arabian Peninsula in the seventh century A.D.)

In the eleventh century, War Jabi, a Takrur king, converted to Islam. This ruler invited an Islamic preacher, Abdullah ibn Yasin, to bring his Takrur subjects into the new faith. Yasin established mosques in Senegal. He also led the Almoravid movement. Almoravid teachers converted large bands of local Berbers and Tuaregs. These nomads wandered the western and northern Sahara, forming a powerful Almoravid army.

The Almoravids conquered the Ghana Empire in 1076. Then they swept northward across the Sahara and as far as Spain. After about fifteen years, Ghana's forces expelled them. Nevertheless, the invasion of the Almoravids seriously disrupted Ghana's vital trade, and the empire began to decline. The authority of the Ghana kings disappeared. Smaller states, including the Wolof Empire, ceased to pay their tribute.

In the twelfth century, the Wolof people were under the control of the Njay dynasty, founded by Njajam Njay. Language and culture united the Wolof states. For two hundred years, the Wolof kings dominated the coastal area. Their territory stretched from the mouth of the Senegal River to modern-day Thiès and as far as 150 miles (241 km) into the interior. Pular speakers continued to rule the middle Senegal River valley. The Malinke controlled the fertile areas of Upper Gambia and the upper reaches of the Senegal River.

In the fourteenth century, the Mali Empire conquered the Wolof realm. The Mali Empire controlled an enormous area including the eastern part of Senegal. The Malinke (also known as the Manninke) migrated into the valley of the Gambia River and eastern Senegal. They forced smaller groups such as the Banun southward into the Casamance region.

Arrival of the Europeans

In the fourteenth century, the Portuguese began sailing to the western coast of Africa. The Europeans were seeking a new trade route to Asia. Portuguese navigators explored the Atlantic Ocean and the island groups that rise along the African coast. They discovered the Madeira Islands off Morocco in 1418. In 1444 the Portuguese explorer Dinis Diaz sailed past the mouth of the Senegal River. His crew made contact with the Wolof realm. From early outposts on Madeira and the Cape Verde Islands (west of Senegal in the Atlantic Ocean), the Portuguese established a profitable trade. They exchanged horses and metal goods for slaves and gold all along the coast of Senegal.

At the same time, conflict within Senegal was weakening the Wolof realm. Smaller tributary states broke away from Wolof control. The dynasty finally collapsed around 1550. This allowed the smaller kingdoms of Sine and Saloum, in western Senegal, to become independent states. Meanwhile, the empire of Mali was also weakening. By the end of the sixteenth century, the Songhai Empire had replaced Mali as the dominant power in Senegal.

Trade and Early Settlement

Until about 1550, the Portuguese controlled the western African coast. Gradually, however, merchants from Holland, France, and Great Britain began to make their claims. By 1617 the Dutch had established settlements on the island of Gorée. A decline in Portuguese military strength helped spur this competition. At the same time, Portuguese merchants were turning their attention to more profitable trading posts. These included the East Indies (modern India and Indonesia) and the Portuguese colony of Brazil in South America.

In the seventeenth century, the French began to exert their influence along the Senegal River. French explorers made their way up the valley, making contact with local kings. In 1626 several French merchants formed the Compagnie du Sénégal (the Senegal Company) for trade along the Senegal and Gambia rivers. The French established Saint-Louis in 1658 on an island at the mouth of the Senegal River. For the next 150 years, Saint-Louis was the base of all French activity and expansion in western Africa. In 1677 the French also captured Gorée from the Dutch and turned it into a naval base.

Within Senegal and Gambia, France and Great Britain fought for control of trade throughout the eighteenth century. The French had outposts at Saint-Louis and Gorée. They sent expeditions to the interior to build new trading stations. The British held the mouth of the Gambia River. Neither European power was able to eliminate the presence of the other. Eventually, the French held Senegal and the British controlled Gambia.

The Slave Trade

Slavery existed within African societies before the arrival of European traders. For centuries the western African kingdoms had carried out slave

A **European trader bargains for water** with the leader of a village on Gorée in 1695. The island was the last stop for many ships before the long trip to Europe or the Americas.

trade with North African realms. But the demand for slaves increased rapidly as European colonies in the New World multiplied. The plantations in these colonies needed cheap labor. Slaves did the heavy labor of harvesting cash crops such as sugar, cotton, indigo, and tobacco.

The region surrounding the Gambia River provided one-third of the slaves captured and sold up to the beginning of the seventeenth century. In the Sahel region, slave traders brought their captives to Bakel, on the eastern border of modern-day Senegal, where a large slave market operated. From this point, slaves were shipped to Gorée and other stations on the Atlantic coast. Some slaves were brought to the Canary Islands and the Azores, Portuguese possessions in the Atlantic Ocean. Others made the long and hard journey to the Americas.

In the 1770s, the Islamic reformer Sulaiman Bal led an Islamic revolution against the pagan chiefs who ruled in Senegal. His followers established a new confederation (union) known as the *almamate.* Muslim clerics and marabouts (teachers) founded this religious state. The almamate organized society into a series of clans. An elected leader, the *almamy,* and councils governed the almamate. They defied the authority of the French and all other outsiders.

The almamate movement opposed the chiefs and aristocracy of the Senegalese kingdoms. Almamate states thrived on slavery and trade with the Europeans and held to their traditional religious beliefs. In 1776 another Islamic leader, Abdul Qadir, banned the export of slaves from areas controlled by the almamate. But the wealthy slave traders

Built in 1776 by the Dutch, Gorée's **House of Slaves** was the last stop before slave ships transported Africans to plantations in the Americas.

opposed the measure. Armed with firearms supplied by the French, the slave traders crushed the revolt. This event placed the coastal region and the Senegal River valley firmly under French control.

French Colonization

At first the French settlements in Senegal served as commercial bases. In the meantime, Africa drew more attention from other European nations. These nations were seeking new sources of raw materials to fuel their expanding industries. They also wanted markets for their goods. An important event in this process was the Congress of Vienna in 1815. At the congress, the European powers recognized the French claim to Senegal.

Through the early nineteenth century, French settlers in search of profitable land to farm moved to western Africa. Along with them came members of the Roman Catholic Church. The church established missions, at which priests preached the Catholic form of Christianity. In 1816 the first French mission school opened its doors in Saint-Louis. In 1840 the French government decreed Senegal a permanent French possession. France established a new administration in Senegal. This administration controlled towns and trading stations along the coast and in the valley of the Gambia River. Traditional chiefs still ruled without interference in the Sahel, the Ferlo region, and in the more remote areas of southern and eastern Senegal.

In 1848 the French government abolished the export of slaves from the colony. Everyone born in the colony had full French citizenship. France set up local councils to govern the settlements. A judicial system using the French law code began trying civil and criminal cases. A few Senegalese (those who satisfied certain educational requirements) had the right to vote for a deputy. The deputy sat in the national legislature in Paris, France. Four years later, however, a new regime came to power in France. This government revoked Senegal's right to a representative.

The growing French control of trade, administration, and justice weakened the traditional African dynasties in Senegal. Many chiefs took up posts within the colonial government. Islamic leaders and teachers became authority figures among the local people. By the middle of the nineteenth century, many of the Wolof had abandoned their animist beliefs and converted to Islam.

The rivalries among the traditional chiefs brought frequent clashes and a constant state of tension. In 1850 al-Haj Omar emerged as a leader of the Tijaniya. The Tijaniya lived in small communities and followed a strict code of Islamic belief and daily ritual. Under the leadership of their marabouts, this group organized a violent revolt against French merchants and farmers.

To deal with the situation, France turned to an experienced military leader, General Louis-Léon-César Faidherbe. France appointed him governor of the colony in 1854. Faidherbe led a well-disciplined volunteer corps of African soldiers, known as the Tirailleurs Sénégalais (Senegalese Riflemen). This force moved up and down the Senegal River valley. They quelled disturbances and enlisted indigenous (native) rulers to their side. Under French commanders, the riflemen were later to achieve international fame.

At the same time, Faidherbe laid the foundations of a prosperous and well-administered colony. He divided the colony into the districts of Saint-Louis, Bakel, and Gorée. Local chiefs appointed by the French administration governed smaller precincts known as *cercles*. An official newspaper, *Le Moniteur du Sénégal* (The Senegal Monitor), began publication in 1855. The founding of the Bank of Senegal soon followed.

To build a modern port and trade depot, the French founded the city of Dakar in 1857. Faidherbe also signed a peace agreement with al-Haj Omar in 1860. In 1871 Senegal again gained the right to send a representative to the French legislature in Paris.

In Senegal the development of state schools made education widely available to Africans. Scholarships gave them the chance to continue training in France. This created a French-educated elite that helped the colony prosper. Among many African Senegalese, however, storytelling and music continued to serve as a means of learning shared customs and national history. The griot was a nomadic performer who recounted tales of heroic deeds and powerful kingdoms. The poetry and songs of the griots remained a vital link to the past for the Mandinka and other peoples.

Striving to bring more territory under their control, the French sent expeditions farther east. The goal of these campaigns was to link

Senegal with trading routes across the Sahara and in the Niger River valley to create a unified western African colony.

The Late Nineteenth Century

Trade between African groups and the French proceeded peaceably. But French occupation of villages met widespread resistance. As the French penetrated farther into the Senegalese interior, they encountered the Takrur realm ruled by Seku Ahmadu from 1864 to 1893. The Takrur forces put up strong resistance. In addition, the Wolof kingdoms struggled against French occupation. This conflict lasted until the death of Wolof leader Lat Jor in 1886.

After the elimination of these two leaders, most of Senegal came under French control. In the Casamance, however, the Jola and other groups continued to fight the French. Clashes broke out regularly for several decades afterward.

An important event in African history was the Berlin Conference of 1884–1885. The nations of Europe met to divide up Africa and claim their rights to African colonies. They had little regard for traditional African homelands or the territorial claims of African leaders.

After the conference, France set out to conquer more territory in western Africa. Senegal served the French as a military and

Senegalese workers and French supervisors rest on a cart at a railroad yard around 1884. By this time, France had administrative control of Senegal.

administrative base. From the strategic port of Dakar, the French administration controlled Senegal as well as Mali and Mauritania.

By 1900 the French had planted their flag across most of western Africa. French colonies also existed in North Africa. France claimed land eastward and southward as far as the Congo region of central Africa.

To govern this territory, France organized the Federation of French West Africa. In 1904 the French detached southern and eastern sections of Senegal to form French Sudan (modern Mali). In 1920 the territory north of the Senegal River became Mauritania.

During the 1930s, Senegalese workers organized to demand better working conditions and legal rights. The Senegalese Socialist Party (PSS, the Frency acronym) formed in 1934. This party modeled itself on European Socialist groups. In a Socialist system, governments own and control the means of production. Socialism grew popular among Africans seeking further independence from European colonial governments.

● Toward Independence

In 1939 World War II broke out in Europe. In the next year, Nazi Germany invaded France. The French government lost territory and control of their government to the Germans.

The fall of France led to the creation of a pro-Nazi government in Vichy, France. Marshal Philippe Pétain led this government. A difficult decision faced French officials and troops in Africa. They could support the Vichy government in France. Or they could pledge loyalty to the Free French forces, who worked in exile under General Charles de Gaulle.

The governor-general of French West Africa and all the governors under him declared their loyalty to the Vichy government. In 1940 British and Free French ships attacked the port of Dakar. This attack failed, and Dakar remained an ally of Vichy France. In 1945, however, Germany lost the war. De Gaulle and the Free French forces reclaimed France and control of the colonies.

After the war, France changed its colonial policies. French and African politicians put forth various proposals. Liberals wanted Africans to have the full rights of French citizenship, including the right to sit in the French National Assembly. Conservatives wanted to extend only certain legal rights and the right of representation in the assembly to the French African colonists.

In 1946 liberals and conservatives reached a compromise. This gave the colonies membership in the newly created French Union, which included France and all of its overseas territories. The agreement guaranteed the African peoples more representation in Paris.

At this time, the Senegalese Socialist Party was seeking to legalize trade unions for workers' rights. A young PSS member named Léopold Sédar Senghor broke away from the party. Senghor formed the Senegalese Democratic Bloc in 1948. The new party urged the French government to increase funds to Senegal for education and health facilities. After it merged with the Socialists in 1958, the Senegalese Democratic Bloc was renamed the Senegalese Progressive Union (UPS).

The New Nation

In 1959, after long negotiations, Senegal and French Sudan decided to merge, forming the independent Mali Federation. Reluctantly, France agreed to accept this arrangement. Rivalries and disagreements between the Senegalese and the Malians caused the new federation to fail. In 1960 Senegal declared itself an independent republic. Former French Sudan retained the name Mali for itself.

Léopold Senghor, who had emerged as a pivotal figure in Senegalese politics in the 1950s, became president of the newly independent Republic of Senegal. Senghor ruled in cooperation with Prime Minister Mamadou Dia. Although Dia was an ally of Senghor, he favored a purely Socialist economy, with the government completely in control of the economy. Following Socialist principles, Senegal placed several major industries under state control. In addition, the government operated all print and broadcast media.

Instead of trying to confront opposition movements within his country, Senghor made alliances with them. But in December 1962, Mamadou Dia attempted a coup (overthrow) of Senghor's administration. The coup failed, and Senghor ordered Dia's arrest. Senegal adopted a new constitution, which

Léopold Sédar Senghor and his wife, Colette, stand for an official presidential portrait in 1960.

increased the president's authority. In 1967 Senghor escaped an attempted assassination. As a result of this, the government arrested and imprisoned many of his political opponents.

In 1974 Senegal celebrated the fourteenth anniversary of independence. Senghor announced an amnesty (forgiveness) for all political prisoners. Two years later, Senegal's lawmakers began reviewing the national constitution. Three political parties emerged from this process. The Socialist Party (PS) represented Senghor and the former Senegalese Progressive Union. Abdoulaye Wade led the Senegalese Democratic Party (PDS). The PDS announced that it followed a liberal program, with open elections, a free-market economic system, and respect for free speech and human rights. Maihemout Diop took charge of the Marxist African Party for Independence (PAI). This party favored a government modeled after the Soviet Union (fifteen republics that included Russia). The one-party government would own all property and industry.

Senegal went through an economic decline in the 1970s. A rise in the price of oil led to inflation. The country found itself struggling with heavy debts to foreign banks. Senghor came under pressure to carry out drastic reforms. Instead, on December 31, 1980, he resigned his office and turned over his duties to Prime Minister Abdou Diouf.

Senghor still held widespread respect among African leaders. He remained active in pursuing a long-held goal of African unity, in which the nations of Africa would form closer political and economic ties. This began with the creation in February 1982 of the Senegambian Confederation. This new state included Gambia, the Casamance region, and the rest of Senegal. It would allow Senegalese ships to make free use of the Gambia River, which would help the country's trade. However, the union proved difficult to govern. It would only last seven years.

In February 1983, 80 percent of the voters chose the PS candidate Diouf as president. He had defeated four opponents. Eight different political parties put up candidates for election to the legislature. Senegal passed new economic measures to control rising prices. The government put price controls on basic goods.

At this time, Senegal was facing a growing separatist movement in the Casamance. The Diola people, who made up a majority in western Casamance, did not want to be ruled by the Wolof majority in the rest of Senegal. The region drew little investment from private companies or the administration in Dakar. Many people of the Casamance wanted their own independent government.

Rebels formed the Movement of Democratic Forces of Casamance to fight for independence. The conflict sparked civil unrest and several battles. There were also kidnappings, terrorism, and murder. In

December 1983, confrontations in Casamance between protesters and police left more than twenty people dead.

During the national elections of 1988, political activists challenged PS power. Some parties increased their representation in the legislature. Nevertheless, Diouf and the PS won by a majority of 73 percent. On election night, young Senegalese participated in street violence. The disturbances prompted the PS government to declare a state of emergency. The government also jailed Abdoulaye Wade, leader of the PDS and one of the main opposition candidates. Wade soon won his release and then left the country. He returned two years later.

In the meantime, ethnic conflict was brewing between Mauritanians and Senegalese along their mutual border. In the capital, many Senegalese protested Mauritanian control of a large number of businesses. The tension flared in April 1989 as full-scale riots broke out in Dakar. Senegalese looted and burned the shops and homes of Mauritanians.

In reprisal, Mauritanians killed more than two hundred Senegalese in the Mauritanian capital of Nouakchott. Airlifts brought terrified ethnic Senegalese to Dakar from Mauritania. Several hundred opponents of Mauritania's regime joined the refugees.

Recent Events

During the 1990s, Senegal took steps to reform its stagnant economy. The state dropped its price controls on cement, coffee, and other goods. Senegal also ended state monopolies on the production of cement, fertilizers, flour, and textiles. The state sold many businesses to private owners and foreign investors.

Senegal still had a heavy load of debt to foreign banks and governments. To improve the situation, the country borrowed from the International Monetary Fund (IMF). The IMF is a financial organization that assists developing countries. It helped Senegal pay its debts and plan a careful spending budget. The result was a drop in inflation. An upswing in economic growth continued into the twenty-first century.

Abdoulaye Wade

In March 2000, Abdoulaye Wade defeated Abdou Diouf. This victory ended four decades of PS control. In the following year, Senegal amended its constitution. The new system allowed for presidential elections every five years, rather than seven. The new system would begin with the end of Wade's first term.

The early years of Wade's term saw a growing rivalry between the president and the prime minister. Wade had appointed PDS leader Idrissa Seck as prime minister in 2002. But Seck was soon

▲ **Senegalese boy from Casamance** watches his family's belongings in a refugee camp. He and thousands of others fled their homes because of rebel violence.

facing accusations of bribery and corruption. These charges embarrassed and angered Wade, who in 2004 dismissed Seck from his post. In the next year, Wade ordered the police to arrest Seck on charges of corruption and for posing a threat to national security. The government eventually dropped the charges. Seck gained widespread support as an opponent of Wade's policies.

Wade made a peace treaty with the Casamance rebels a priority of his administration. Although the two sides sat down to negotiate in 2005, they didn't reach an agreement. Wade won reelection in 2007, when Idrissa Seck polled second with 15 percent of the vote.

Senegal has created an open and democratic political system, although violence still occurs. The country gives room to a relatively free press and active trade unions. Students and political leaders state their views openly. In foreign affairs, Senegal maintains friendly relations with countries in Europe, eastern Asia, and the rest of Africa.

KIDS CALL A TIME-OUT!

The Casamance conflict simmers on without an end in sight. Peace talks are on hold. But to try to resolve the conflict, an organization known as World Education is training a new group of peacemakers: kids.

In this program, schools in Casamance are teaching conflict resolution to eighteen thousand students. They learn about the roots of the war, how to negotiate, and the skills of advocacy, including helping people understand their ideas. The students organize peace rallies and friendly soccer matches to bring people of different communities together. Similar programs have been successful in Colombia and the Philippines.

The former colony also keeps close relations with France. President Wade seeks regional cooperation among the countries of western Africa. Following Senghor's policy, he also supports further steps toward African unity.

▶ Government

Senegal adopted its first constitution in 1963. The current constitution, adopted in 2001, gives broad powers to a president. This office lasts for a term of five years. The constitution allows a maximum of two terms. While the president serves as the head of state, the prime minister serves as the head of government. He or she appoints a cabinet (group of advisers) to run the various government departments.

The Parliament of Senegal is a bicameral (two-house) legislature. There are 150 members of the National Assembly. Of these members, voters directly elect 90, while the rest earn seats according to a system of proportional representation. The number of members from each party depends on the percent of the vote won by the parties in the general election. The Senate consists of 100 members. The president appoints 65 members, while the rest are seated according to proportional representation. The legislative and presidential elections take place at the same time.

The **Senegalese National Assembly** meets in this building in Dakar.

Senegal modeled its court system after the French system that was in place when Senegal was a colony. Justices of the peace hear local cases, while courts of first instance handle more serious criminal and civil cases. Assize (criminal) courts hold sessions in the major cities. The Cour de Cassation is the highest court of appeal in Senegal. The president appoints members to this court and to the Constitutional Council. This group decides the constitutionality of laws passed by the legislature.

Women have taken the reins as political leaders in several towns and departments in Senegal. In the early 1960s and just after independence, the Parliament had no female members at all. Currently, it has more than twenty. Mame Madior Baye became the first female prime minister of Senegal in 2001.

Senegal has eleven administrative regions: Dakar, Diourbel, Fatick, Kaolack, Kolda, Louga, Matam, Saint-Louis, Tambacounda, Thiès, and Ziguinchor. The president appoints the governors who head the regions. Local councils administer the regions. The country further divides the regions into a total of thirty-four departments and 103 arrondissements (local administrations).

Visit www.vgsbooks.com for links to websites with additional information about the history and government of Senegal. Tour the island of Gorée, and learn about the country's elected officials.

THE PEOPLE

Senegal's population is about 12.8 million. The country has a population density of about 169 people per square mile (65 per sq. km). Senegal is most crowded in the west, with a belt of cities and towns running eastward from Dakar and northward and southward along the Atlantic Ocean coast.

The country's growth rate of 3 percent a year represents an average rate in western Africa. By the year 2025, the population will reach about 18 million. By 2050, at its current rate of growth, Senegal will have roughly 25.3 million people. In addition, about 44 percent of the Senegalese are under the age of fifteen. This high rate will contribute to future population growth.

Senegal's cities are growing quickly. Many new arrivals come from rural areas where drought, erosion, and deforestation have hurt farming. Farmers often move to the cities during the dry season, when the land cannot be cultivated. Some work for a time and then return home to plant when the rainy season approaches. Nevertheless, a majority of

the population—about 60 percent—still make their permanent homes in rural areas.

Ethnic Groups and Languages

Several ethnic groups inhabit Senegal. For the most part, the groups live peacefully with one another. Senegal experiences only occasional cultural conflicts. The largest ethnic group is the Wolof, who make up nearly 40 percent of the population. The smaller groups include the Fulbé, Serer, Tukulor, Malinke, Jola, and Bassari. As many as one hundred thousand non-Africans—mostly French, Lebanese, and Syrians—also live in Senegal.

The Wolof—known by that name as early as the fifteenth century—originated in the kingdom of Djolof. They gradually dominated other groups, who paid taxes and swore loyalty to the Wolof conquerors. Modern western Africa has a large Wolof population, most of whom live in Senegal, especially in the northern, eastern, and coastal regions and around Dakar.

These **Wolof people** live in a village in northwestern Senegal.

Smaller Wolof communities are in neighboring African countries and in France. In modern Senegal, ethnic Wolof make up about 43 percent of the population. Wolof dominate the country's government, military, and education system. About 90 percent of all Senegalese can understand the Wolof language.

The Pular-speaking peoples include two subdivisions: the Fula and the Tukulor. Historically, the Fula (also known as the Fulani people) were herders. They represent about 24 percent of modern Senegal. Related groups in northern Africa use their language, known as Fula, or Pular. In Senegal most Fula live in the northern part of the country. Other Fula regions are in the Senegal River valley and in the upper Casamance region.

The Tukulor, who compose about 10 percent of the population, live around the Senegal River valley of the north. They are proud of their language, customs, and Muslim religion. The Tukulor raised a long-lasting dynasty in medieval Africa. They strongly resisted foreign culture and government during the colonial era.

A FEW WORDS OF WOLOF

hello	*na nga def*
good-bye	*ba beneen*
please	*su la nexee*
thank you	*jai ru jef*
I'm sorry	*baal ma*
yes	*waau*
no	*deedeet*
How are you?	*jaam nga am?*
What's up?	*maka du?*

The Serer make up about 18 percent of the population. They work as fishers along the coast and as farmers inland in the Saloum and Thiès regions. Through the centuries, they have resisted Islam and held to traditional animist beliefs. In recent years, however, many Serer have converted to Islam. About 10 percent of the Serer profess Christianity. This represents a larger percentage of Christians than in other ethnic groups.

The Malinke speak languages derived from those of the former Mali Empire. They represent around 5 percent of the population of Senegal. Malinke people live in many parts of western Africa, mainly in Guinea, Ivory Coast, Gambia, and Mali. Most of the Malinke are farmers in the upper Casamance region, in Tambacounda, and in southeastern areas of the country.

A number of smaller ethnic groups live in the southern Casamance region and in eastern Senegal. These groups, including the Bassari, Manjak, and Jola, speak languages unrelated to the Niger-Congo languages of Pular, Serer, Wolof, and Malinke. Historically, these peoples resisted conquest by larger kingdoms and empires. As a result, they were a frequent target of slave hunters and other exploiters. They still tend to be suspicious of governmental authority and prefer to remain within their own communities.

Non-Africans live chiefly in urban areas. They are mostly of French, Lebanese, and Syrian descent. During the colonial period, Senegal was the administrative center for French West Africa. French immigrants came as administrators, merchants, and technicians. After independence many of these foreigners kept their administrative and commercial jobs. Most French firms with offices in Senegal employ descendants of French settlers or more recent immigrants from France. Lebanese and Syrian families came to Senegal as merchants and traders from their former homes in the Middle East.

Until independence there was limited social contact between French and Africans. The French excluded the Senegalese from many political and cultural activities. After independence the situation changed. The French no longer

ARABS IN SENEGAL

The French encouraged people from Lebanon and Syria to settle in Senegal during the colonial period. The Lebanese and the Syrians became an important link between rural farmers and urban merchants. They purchased the produce of the villagers, offering them consumer goods in exchange. They resold the produce to merchants or wholesalers in town. The Lebanese were successful in their commercial enterprises. Lebanese families still control a good part of the country's business.

dominate Senegalese politics, and vibrant Senegalese music, art, and literary scenes are thriving. The French, however, still are a major force in Senegalese service industries, such as export businesses and banks. French remains the official language of Senegal. Only a small minority of Senegalese, however, use it on a daily basis. French is useful to Senegalese traveling or doing business in Europe or other parts of western Africa.

Family and Community

Many people in Senegal live among extended families that include several generations. Some ethnic groups are largely matrilineal, meaning they trace descent through the mother. This traditional African system contrasts with patrilineal families, which trace heritage through the father's side. Since the advent of Islam in Senegal, patrilineal families have become more common. Fathers are considered the head of the household, with authority over wives, children, and the family's goods and property. Towns and villages include groups of families that share land and goods in common. These communities live in large compounds and count several households as members. The households care for crops, cattle, and small cottage industries that make goods for sale in the local marketplace.

Polygamy, or the practice of a man having several wives, remains customary in Senegal. It is especially common in villages and rural areas. A first wife holds a position of authority over the household. Other wives live in separate living quarters. Polygamy is less common in urban areas, where members of an extended family tend to live apart from one another.

A **Wolof man stands with his second wife and child** in a village near Thiès.

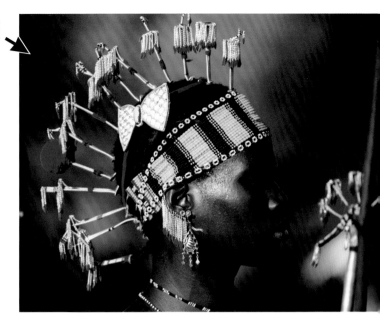

A **woman of the Bassari ethnic group** wears a traditional headdress during a birthday ceremony. Bassari women celebrate a new stage of life every six years.

Women in Senegal

By tradition, women in Senegal take the role of caregivers within the household. They cultivate, plant, and harvest the family's crops. They bring household goods and produce to local markets, where they buy, sell, and trade. It is common for Senegalese women to marry quite young and to remarry quickly in case of divorce or the death of their spouse.

By its constitution, Senegal guarantees equal status before the law for men and women. But until recently, higher education was largely reserved for men. Girls had few opportunities beyond primary school. Many families expected them simply to care for the household until marriage. As a result, the literacy rate is lower for women. Many still contend with discrimination for job opportunities.

While working men draw regular salaries, many women working in factories are paid by the piecework method. They are paid a certain amount for each item or article of clothing they produce. This usually results in lower wages. In addition, piecework laborers have few job benefits such as insurance, vacation, or sick pay. Women also have limited access to bank loans for starting a business of their own. In cities, however, many women have made their way in the white-collar service industries. Women also hold many civil service jobs.

In rural areas, some families select marriage partners for their daughters. These arranged marriages restrict the young women's choices of whom they will marry. Some households are polygamous, in which a man has two or more wives. About half of all women in the country live in polygamous households, where they have no say in the marriage of their husbands to another woman. The Senegalese largely favor big families, and women give birth to children an average of five times during their lives.

In Senegal, women also face a common problem of domestic violence. Few shelters are available for battered women, who often do not wish to involve police or other family members. Some communities also practice female genital mutilation. By this tradition, a crude medical operation scars the sexual organs of young girls. The practice can result in infection, ongoing medical problems, and even death. Some Senegalese are working to end this practice.

Education

Historically, Senegal has provided some form of education to people of varied ethnic background and economic levels. The colony had missionary and private schools, as well as medical schools and a science institute. Nevertheless, in many places, schooling was brief. Many young people did not understand French, the language of instruction, or attain basic skills in reading, writing, or mathematics. After independence the overall literacy rate remained low—about 10 percent.

The government undertook new public investment in facilities, teacher salaries, and books in the 1990s. This helped the school system to expand. Classrooms opened in rural areas and in urban neighborhoods. In the twenty-first century, about 65 percent of school-age children attend primary school, which lasts for six years. Attendance

Students walk home from a **high school in Dakar.** About 15 percent of eligible Senegalese students attend high school.

is lower for the four-year middle school courses. About 15 percent of eligible students attend the three-year high school. The country's over-all literacy rate has reached 40 percent.

Aware of the importance of education, parents are eager to send their children to school, when schools are available. The language barrier, however, still prevents many students from fully realizing their potential. Although Wolof dominates, no single language is universally understood. Many students do not speak or read French—the language of classroom instruction and Senegalese textbooks. In addition, many Senegalese girls stay home and do not attend school. Senegal requires attendance for all children in elementary school. In addition, the country has opened all secondary schools and universities to young women.

Cheikh Anta Diop University, formerly the University of Dakar, offers instruction in the humanities, the sciences, business, law, and medicine. Enrollment has grown to forty thousand students. Space is limited, forcing students to compete for space in crowded classrooms and dormitories. Gaston Berger University in the city of Saint-Louis also offers post-secondary instruction. Another ten thousand students attend vocational schools, which offer training in practical trades.

▶ Health

Many areas of Senegal struggle with inadequate sanitation facilities, poverty, and poor nutrition. Overall, the country's level of health care is substandard, except in Dakar and a few other large towns. A main source of trouble is a shortage of fresh drinking water. Polluted water spreads disease. Many towns lack proper sewage and drainage systems.

Also harmful to the health of the Senegalese are mosquitoes, which transmit the deadly diseases malaria and yellow fever. Tsetse flies carry the virus that causes sleeping sickness. Senegal is struggling with a rising rate of tuberculosis, an infectious lung disease. Along with malaria, tuberculosis is a leading cause of death.

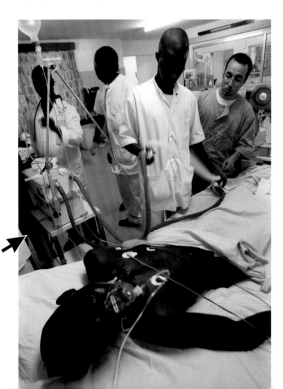

Doctors treat a malaria patient at a hospital in Dakar. Those who live outside of Senegal's cities may struggle to get medical help.

Life expectancy in Senegal is 60 years for males and 64 for females. These are among the highest averages among countries of western Africa, where many nations have even fewer health facilities. Infant mortality has fallen to 61 deaths out of every 1,000 live births. In comparison, the figure in Africa as a whole is estimated to be 86 deaths in each 1,000 live births. In France, however, which once ruled Senegal, fewer than 4 babies per 1,000 births die.

The government is trying to correct unhealthful conditions, but many difficulties exist. Lack of money and trained workers slow progress toward better health standards. There are about six hundred doctors in a country of more than 12 million people, and many rural areas have no trained physicians or clinics.

To make health care more available, the government has set up mobile hospitals and X-ray and laboratory units. These units travel from village to village, providing badly needed medical care. They instruct people about hygiene and forms of preventive medicine.

Senegal has been successful in fighting HIV, the virus that causes AIDS (acquired immunodeficiency syndrome). About 0.7 percent of the population between the ages of fifteen and forty-nine carry the virus. This figure is low in a continent where the average figure has reached 4.5 percent and has been rising steadily. The government encourages its citizens to practice safe sex. It also promotes AIDS education for the young.

THE BROTHERHOODS OF SENEGAL

Many Islamic believers in Senegal belong to religious brotherhoods. These associations date back centuries. The idea came from North Africa, where charismatic marabouts gathered followers and established separate communities. The most important brotherhoods in modern times are the Qadiriya, Tijaniya, Mouridiya, and the Baye Fall.

Religion

About 90 percent of Senegalese are Muslim. This belief system arose in the seventh century in present-day Saudi Arabia. Muslims believe in the holy writings of the Quran as received from God (Allah) by the prophet Muhammad.

About 5 percent of Senegalese—including the late president Léopold Sédar Senghor—are Christian, having adopted the Roman Catholic faith of the French. Colonial schools taught Catholicism, and Catholic missionaries converted many families, especially in urban areas.

Senegalese Muslims have organized traditional Islamic groups called brotherhoods. Their leaders

Members of the Mouridiya, the largest Muslim brotherhood in Senegal, visit the **Great Mosque in the holy city of Touba.**

hold considerable political power within the country. They serve as advisers to politicians and can influence the way their members vote.

Many Senegalese continue to honor traditional beliefs and religious practices, known as animism. These beliefs are present throughout much of sub-Saharan Africa (the vast African region lying south of the Sahara). Animist religions focus on a universal life force that is present in the natural world. Those who practice traditional beliefs seek to control this power for practical ends. For example, believers may hope to ensure a good harvest or to find a job. About 5 percent of Senegal's population supports this belief system. Most of the country's Muslim and Christian populations also accept some elements of these traditional ideas.

Visit www.vgsbooks.com for links to websites with additional information about the people of Senegal. Learn about different ethnic groups, and listen to samples of languages spoken in Senegal.

CULTURAL LIFE

Both African and European traditions have inspired modern Senegal's art and culture. When the nation was a colony of France, a new language arrived along with the influence of European writers, artists, and musicians. French-language schools and media gave the people a widely understood basis for communication. The Catholic Church and its missionary schools converted many Senegalese to a new religion.

In modern times, President Senghor led a rebellion against the dominance of Francophone (French-speaking) culture. Senghor advanced the idea of Negritude. This outlook placed African culture on an equal footing with that of Europe. Senghor and like-minded artists and writers, as well as historians, brought African traditions and style to the forefront. The government gave generous support to Senegalese artists and cultural institutions. The result was one of Africa's most vibrant artistic scenes.

Senegal's artists draw notice around the world. In the capital of

Dakar, the Daniel Soreno Theater hosts important performances. The IFAN Museum presents African art, including sculpture, jewelry, and masks. These institutions, along with the world-renowned musicians and singers, make Senegal a cultural leader among African nations.

Music and Dance

Dance and music have long been Senegal's most important forms of artistic expression. In the past, ritual dances developed as part of religious or ethnic ceremonies. These elaborate performances still take place in modern Senegal.

Senegalese dances are expressive, allowing a great deal of spontaneous movement within certain traditional forms. Emphasis is placed on group participation rather than on individual performance. Chanting and musical instruments, especially drums and *balaphons* (xylophones), serve as accompaniment. The *sabar*, a traditional "talking drum," provides an expressive and melodious beat for performers.

Griots recount legends and histories to the accompaniment of a musical instrument. Many griot traditions date to the Mali Empire and songs of praise performed at the courts of the Malian kings. The griot learns his profession from family elders and has a favored place among performers. Griots wander through a region, creating spontaneous commentaries or satirical works on current events.

Senegal also takes pride in a lively modern musical scene. Popular music has roots in orchestras that performed at Dakar's many nightclubs and concert venues. The Star Band, led by Ibra Kassa, brought popular music from the United States and Cuba to Senegal. Many groups followed, including Orchestra Baobab and the Super Etoile de Dakar (Star of Dakar), led by Youssou N'Dour.

In recent years, Senegal's musical offerings have gained an international audience. Youssou N'Dour and Super Etoile de Dakar have appeared in concerts in the United States and Great Britain. N'Dour popularized *mbalax*, a dance music that fuses jazz, soul, salsa, and rock. The songs of Baaba Maal describe the scattering of his fellow Tukulor throughout western Africa. Maal and his band Dande Lenol mix jazz, reggae, Cuban salsa, and blues in a distinctly African way. Positive Black Soul and the Afro-Celt Sound System have adopted the rap and hip-hop style popular in the United States.

THE MBALAX SOUND

The exciting sound of mbalax began when musicians combined traditional sabar drumming of western Africa with Cuban salsa and rumba beats. Later mbalax groups adopted jazz and funk from the United States, while adding the electric guitar, horn sections, and electric keyboards.

Mbalax music dates to the 1970s, when the writers, artists, and musicians of Senegal were following President Senghor's idea of Negritude, which raised African traditions above those imported by outsiders during the colonial era. Youssou N'Dour and his band Etoile de Dakar wrote the music's first hits. The steady beat of the *mbungmbung* drum gave the genre its new name, although some new groups use a rhythm guitar to create a similar sound.

The biggest mbalax stars are Thione Seck, Omar Pene, and Lamine Faye. But in Senegal, just about every band that performs in public has a few mbalax numbers in its playbook.

Youssou N'Dour performs in Dakar.

Literature

Until Muslim traders brought Arabic writing to Senegal, there was no written language. Consequently, only oral literature existed, mostly in the form of storytelling. The most famous storytellers in Senegal are the griots, who as poets and entertainers play an important role in recording historical events. The eighteenth-century poet Phillis Wheatley, who was brought as a slave from Senegal to North America, became the first African woman to publish her works in the Americas.

French-educated Senegalese writers have produced a large number of novels, short stories, and essays. A common theme in these works is the defense of African culture against the powerful influences of Europe. Many Senegalese books have appeared in English in the United States.

Amadou Mapate, a schoolteacher, wrote a famous tale titled *Le Trois Volontés de Malic* (Malic's Three Wishes) during the 1920s. Bakari Diallo wrote *Force-Bonté* (The force of goodwill) about the life of a Senegalese *tirailleur*, or rifleman. The Senegalese novelist and filmmaker Ousmane Sembene combines a distinctive writing style with strong political ideas. His major work, *Les Bouts de Bois de Dieu* (God's Bits of Wood) retraces the 1947–1948 strike of the workers in the Dakar-Bamako Railway.

Ousmane Sembene

Among the country's other leading literary figures are the poets David Diop and former president Léopold Sédar Senghor, who was a world-renowned poet before he became the Senegalese president. Senghor's idea of Negritude placed the best creative works of Africans alongside the most renowned works of Europe. Senghor believed in a distinctly African voice and feeling and in the contribution of African societies to ancient Greece, Rome, and the values of Europe.

Senegal's leading modern writers include the novelists Abdoulaye Sadji, Ousmane Soce, and Mariama Bâ, who broke onto the literary scene with her book *So Long a Letter*. The historian Cheikh Anta Diop is known around the world for his challenging concepts of African history and culture. Boubacar Boris Diop, a leading contemporary writer, founded the newspaper *Sol* and wrote *Murambi: The Book of Remains* about the Rwandan genocide of 1994. In 2006 Diop also published the first Wolof novel, *Doomi Golo*.

Arts and Crafts

The support of arts by the government of Senegal allows art and visual media to flourish. The École des Beaux Arts (School of Fine Arts) in Dakar and the annual World Festival of Black Arts bring many skilled artists to the fore, including Ibn N'Diaye, Mor Faye, Ibou Diouf, Papa Ibra Tall, and Ousmane Faye. These and other artists helped to found a twentieth-century Dakar School of art, which combined European and African themes.

Senegal also has a long tradition of craftmaking, which includes media common in the rest of Africa: musical instruments, leatherwork, tapestries, gold and silver jewelry, wooden masks and carvings, and pottery. Senegalese artists have developed new art forms, including the technique of *souwere* (a word that comes from the French term *sous-verre*, or "under glass"). This technique of glass painting came from North Africa in the early twentieth century. The earliest examples depicted individuals and events from Islamic history. Later artists are adapting them to everyday life, folktales, portraits, and natural scenes. The souwere serves some of the country's leading artists, including Gora M'Bengue, as a principal medium of expression.

Modern and traditional wood carvings mingle at a craft market in Dakar.

Senegalese soccer player Babacar Gueye (right) races an Algerian player for the ball at a tournament in Dakar.

Sports and Recreation

The most popular team sport in Senegal is football (soccer), played on pitches large and small throughout the country. A professional league plays a long season, while Senegal also plays against opponents that come from other parts of Africa. Senegal takes pride in fielding one of the best national teams in Africa. Nicknamed the Lions of Teranga, the team advanced to the quarterfinals in the 2002 World Cup, after beating defending champion France in the first round of the tournament.

Traditional wrestling also enjoys a mass following. Most Senegalese wrestlers appear in neighborhood arenas, while the best-known grapple in national stadiums such as the Iba Mar Diop Stadium in Dakar. Music, chants, and dancing accompany the wrestlers to the ring. They fight with no holds barred to bring one another to the ground. A team of judges decides the high-stakes professional matches, which reward the victors with substantial prizes.

Senegal also has a basketball league and a top-rated national team. The country has sent several players to the National Basketball Association, including DeSagana Diop of Dakar, who played for the Dallas Mavericks in 2007–2008. Since the 1970s, Senegal has won five gold medals in the FIBA Africa Championships. The women's team has taken first, second, or third place in every FIBA women's tournament since 1967.

Popular recreational sports include offshore diving, sport fishing, hiking, and trekking in the country's large national parks. Senegal also hosts the finish of the Dakar Rally, formerly the Paris-Dakar, a grueling road race from Europe through the Sahara. In this dangerous event, hundreds of off-road vehicles cross sand, rock, and desert mountains.

Food

The Senegalese diet varies according to what foods are available locally. Along the coast and rivers, fish is served in many different forms. A favorite national dish is fish stew, made with several varieties of fresh fish, sea snails, dried fish, and vegetables seasoned with hot peppers. Tropical fruits, such as oranges, mangoes, bananas, and coconuts, are also available along the coast. Wherever irrigation is possible, okra, green peppers, tomatoes, and eggplants are grown in small gardens. For those living inland, the staple diet consists of starchy cereals such as millet, sorghum, corn, and rice. These items are pounded in large wooden bowls and then boiled to varying thicknesses and seasoned with different spices.

Because the typical Senegalese diet is high in starches and low in animal proteins and calcium, it is not always sufficiently nutritious. Milk and meat products are rare, except in large cities and among the Fulbé, who own herds of cattle. Meat is seldom eaten, except in the form of chicken or lamb stew.

A breakfast in Senegal can include bread in the form of a French baguette; yogurt mixed with millet,

THREE ROUNDS OF TEA

Attaya is a tea-drinking tradition in Senegal. Hosts serve cups of tea in three rounds. To prepare *lewel*, or the first round, the host combines *warga*, or tea leaves, with a little bit of sugar and brings to a boil. The tea is poured into glasses and then back into the pot. When it is finally served, it is strong and bitter. For the second round, mint leaves and sugar go into the pot again. For the last and sweetest round, the host pours even more sugar and mint, sometimes adding mint candy. Like friendship, the attaya ceremony is more fun—and sweeter—the longer it lasts.

A man prepares the traditional tea, *attaya*, in a village in Senegal.

sugar, beans, or peanuts; and coffee. Peanuts and cassava chips are popular daytime snacks. In the streets and markets, food stalls offer snacks and meat dishes, cooked to order on small charcoal grills. For the main evening meal at home, families gather around a common bowl of rice or millet, accompanied by vegetables in season and meat or fish, if available.

The Senegalese have a varied cuisine, which includes ingredients and recipes from Europe and throughout the African continent. One favorite is the North African dish of couscous, which is made of steamed semolina or millet grain and a hot stew of meat and tomatoes, onions, beans, and other vegetables. *Yassa* is chicken served with lemons or a lemon sauce, while *thiou au poulet* is a chicken stew. Many popular dishes, including *mate aux arachid*, are cooked with *mafe*, or peanut sauce. *Thieboudienne*, sometimes called the national dish, mixes fried or boiled fish with vegetables, potatoes, and rice.

MAFE (PEANUT BUTTER STEW)

½ cup creamy peanut butter

2 cups beef broth

2 pounds beef stew meat, cut into 1½-inch cubes

salt and pepper

2 tablespoons vegetable oil

1 cup chopped onion

3–4 cloves minced garlic

1 cup chopped green bell pepper

1 cup chopped carrots

14.5-ounce can diced tomatoes and the liquid

½ teaspoon dried thyme

1 bay leaf

1. In a medium bowl, whisk together the peanut butter and the beef broth until well blended. Set aside.
2. Season the meat with salt and pepper, and set aside.
3. In a large saucepan or stew pot, heat the vegetable oil over medium heat.
4. Add the onion, garlic, bell pepper, and carrots. Sauté until the onions are translucent. Add the meat, and continue to cook, stirring often, until it is browned on all sides.
5. Add the peanut butter and broth mixture, tomatoes and liquid, thyme, and bay leaf. Stir well and bring to a boil. Reduce heat to low and simmer, stirring often for about 1 hour or until the meat is tender.
6. Taste, and add salt and pepper, if desired. Remove the bay leaf and discard.

Serve hot over rice.

Serves 6.

Holidays and Festivals

Senegal has a full calendar of public holidays, including New Year's Day, Labor Day (May 1), and Independence Day (April 4). This holiday celebrates the independence of Senegal in 1960 with street parades, pageants, and athletic events such as canoe races in the Senegal River. On July 14, the African Community Day, or the Day of Association, takes place. This holiday celebrates African unity and culture.

The Islamic New Year's Day is known as Tamxarit and takes place shortly after January 1. On this day, Muslims remember the flight of the prophet Muhammad from the city of Mecca. The birthday of Muhammad, known as Mouloud, is celebrated on March 20. Ramadan takes place during the ninth month of the Islamic calendar. This holiday commemorates the month when the Quran was first revealed to Muhammad. Out of respect, Muslims neither eat nor drink from sunset to sunrise, are devoted to prayer, and avoid all worldly pleasures, including music and sex. At the end of Ramadan (Eid al-Fitr, or Korité), the fasting is broken amid much celebration.

The Grand Magal pilgrimage and celebration is held forty-eight days after the Islamic New Year in the holy city of Touba. It commemorates the return from exile of Sheikh Amadou Bamba, the illustrious founder of the Mouridiya brotherhood, and attracts about two million devotees.

Muslims pray at an outdoor mosque in Dakar during a religious festival.

Catholics pray and light candles at a **shrine in the village of Popenguine** on the Christian holiday of Pentecost.

Christian holidays include Good Friday (which marks the death of Jesus) and Easter Sunday, when by tradition Jesus rose from the dead. Ascension, which takes place forty days after, celebrates Jesus' ascent into heaven. Other public Christian holidays include Whit (Pentecost) Monday, Assumption, All Saints' Day, and Christmas. On Pentecost, the seventh Sunday after Easter, Senegalese Catholics make a pilgrimage to the small fishing village of Popenguine. The village holds an important shrine, said to be the place where the Virgin Mary was once sighted.

Visit www.vgsbooks.com for links to websites with additional information about the culture of Senegal. Listen to samples of mbalax music, and try recipes for Senegalese food.

THE ECONOMY

In the 2000s, Senegal has improved its economy. The government has privatized—sold to private investors—some publicly owned companies. This practice brings money into the public treasury and reduces budget deficits. It also makes public administration more efficient. In addition, Senegal has benefited from debt relief. Many foreign governments and banks have reduced the amount of money Senegal owes.

Senegal is more prosperous than some western African countries. Yet many economic problems still trouble its people. The nation has relied heavily on a single crop, peanuts. For more than three decades, peanuts have been the principal export. Inadequate farming methods, low soil fertility, drought, and locusts (grasshoppers) have also plagued Senegalese agriculture. Unemployment is high in Dakar and many other cities. A small manufacturing sector does not provide enough urban jobs.

Adding to these troubles is Senegal's dependence on international markets for essential items, such as fuel and rice, which have become

increasingly expensive. A worldwide shortage of rice that began in 2008 struck the country hard. Many Senegalese found themselves unable to afford this staple item. The rising cost of gasoline has made basic goods more expensive.

Senegal's gross domestic product (GDP)—the total value of goods and services produced within the country—rose nearly 5 percent per year in the early years of the twenty-first century. That rate increased to 6.2 percent in 2005. Senegal found a welcoming market in Europe for its fish and farm products. The country also developed a thriving tourism industry.

◉ Services

Services contribute about 64 percent of Senegal's GDP, making it the largest sector of the national economy. Banking, insurance, foreign trade, and retail businesses all generate large amounts of income. Services employ 18 percent of the workforce. Senegal draws large foreign investments in the service sector. Asian and European companies are seeking a foothold in the growing market in western Africa.

Tourism has been a mainstay of the Senegalese economy since independence. This business benefits the country by drawing in foreign exchange. Tourism has less of an environmental impact than heavy industry, mining, and agriculture. New resorts and hotels on the coast employ thousands of staff workers and construction laborers. The country's beaches attract large crowds of European visitors each summer. Those who enjoy natural settings visit the country's six national parks. Dakar offers the Dak'Art Biennale, a citywide arts festival, and the Festival Mondial des Arts Nègres, a huge celebration of African music.

Manufacturing, Mining, and Energy

Senegalese industry, mining, and energy contributed about 19 percent of GDP in 2004. These industries combined employ 5 percent of the workforce. The city of Dakar and the surrounding region have the majority of working factories. Most of these plants serve the agricultural sector, with food processing concerns supplying packaged goods, beverages, fish, meat, flour, and sugar to the domestic market. A key sector is peanut-oil processing, which alone accounts for about 25 percent of the total industrial output. Senegalese companies also manufacture cement, shoes, textiles, chemicals, paper, furniture, and electrical products.

Senegal is seeking joint manufacturing ventures with foreign countries. China has negotiated joint ventures in Senegal and throughout western Africa. In 2008 an Iranian company, Samand, began producing automobiles in a new factory in Thiès.

The Senegalese decorative arts cooperative factory in Thiès that makes world-famous tapestries. Artists design the tapestries as paintings. Skilled weavers re-create the designs on looms. The process of weaving is very slow—only about 11 sq. feet (1 sq. m) of a tapestry is finished in a month. The cooperative sells the expensive tapestries to collectors around the world, and diplomats from Senegal often give them to heads of state as gifts.

Senegal's mining industry is concentrated in the more accessible western part of the country. Some exploratory operations are at work in eastern Senegal to search for deposits of zinc, copper, and lead. The coastal zone has large quantities of titanium-filled sand, which yields zircon, a mineral used in gem making. Large rock deposits contain calcium phosphate, which is a valuable

Young gold miners walk past mine shafts covered with branches in eastern Senegal. Children in the mines labor in dangerous conditions.

source of fertilizer. Limestone, used in cement manufacturing, is abundant in the Rufisque area.

Petroleum deposits exist off the coast of the Casamance region, and natural gas has been found near Dakar, although Senegal is still seeking foreign investment to exploit these energy sources. In all, mining contributed about 1 percent of GDP. Energy businesses generate power and refine crude oil into petroleum. These industries make up about 7 percent of GDP.

A key component of the power system, the Manatali Dam, was built in Mali on the Bafing River, a tributary of the Senegal River, in the 1980s. Currently about one-third of Senegal's electric power comes from this and other hydroelectric sources. As the economy and population grow, however, SENELEC, the national electricity company, is still grappling with shortages of fuel and with regular power outages. To help solve these problems, Senegal is building a diesel fuel plant at Kounoune, near Dakar.

Agriculture and Fishing

In the early 1970s, Senegal experienced a severe drought. This disaster hit many other countries in the Sahel region. The country's chief crop—peanuts—suffered heavy damage. Livestock died in large numbers as streams and pastures dried up. The United Nations conducted a large-scale relief effort to distribute foodstuffs. Rainfall levels rose in 1985, which helped to ease the poor growing conditions.

Women harvest rice on a farm on the Saloum River.

The agricultural sector in Senegal is still recovering from the effects of the Sahel drought. Only about half the arable land is under cultivation. To provide a reliable water supply, new irrigation projects are under construction.

Agriculture contributed about 17 percent of GDP in 2005 and employed 77 percent of the labor force. Peanuts still make up about half of the total agricultural production and account for 30 to 50 percent of the country's export earnings. Peanut growing was a state-run monopoly until 1985. Nevertheless, only half of the revenue from peanut exports went to the growers. The other half was meant as a safeguard against famine years. The money, however, actually funded government projects or supported the administrative bureaucracy in Dakar.

Millet and sorghum, raised in northern and central Senegal, supply the domestic market. Growers raise rice, which demands plentiful water, in the Senegal River valley. In recent years, cotton has become a promising new cash crop, and the success of experimental plantings has encouraged cultivation on a larger scale. Other important crops include flowers for export, as well as sugarcane, corn, cassava (a fleshy root crop), and beans. Senegal is not self-sufficient in foodstuffs, and the nation must import a large amount of grain and other foods.

Farmers cultivate garden vegetables—such as watermelons, squash, okra, eggplants, tomatoes, and peppers—along the coast. Farther inland, however, these crops grow on a very small scale, mostly for home consumption. The oil palm, which grows wild, provides palm oil, a basic ingredient in western African cooking.

The tobacco crop provides small quantities for home use. Tropical fruits—mangoes, coconuts, and citrus fruits—are raised along the coast but not in large enough amounts for export. In more remote areas, many wild products, such as wild honey and the leaf and fruit of the baobab tree, supplement the Senegalese diet.

Livestock raising is not a major factor in the economy of the country, despite the fairly large number of cattle, sheep, goats, horses, donkeys, and camels in Senegal. To many Fulbé, however, cattle raising represents a way of life, although the animals are considered more as symbols of dignity and personal status than as the means of financial gain. During the dry season and when droughts occur, the Fulbé travel great distances to supply their herds with water.

PIROGUE-ING IT

Many people living on the coast or along Senegal's rivers use the slender but sturdy pirogue to get around. A pirogue is handy for fishing or for transporting people and goods over calm waters. It looks like a long canoe, with the bigger ones needing several oars to drive them forward. The base of the pirogue is made from a hollowed-out tree trunk, which has been dried and cured for sealing. Wooden planks coated with waterproof tar make up the sides.

With its long Atlantic coastline, Senegal recently has concentrated on expanding its fishing industry. Traditionally, this industry operated on a small scale. Many villages that line the Atlantic coast depend on fishing for a basic food supply. Tuna, oysters, lobsters, and shrimp are plentiful in these coastal waters, although overfishing is depleting this valuable resource.

Fishers prepare their boats at a beach near Dakar. These modern boats are descendants of traditional canoes.

Since the acquisition of modern fishing vessels, fishing has become a more important enterprise in Senegal. Foreign experts have assisted Senegal in developing modern, scientific fishing methods. The industry employs over ten thousand people. Much of the fish is canned for export and for shipment to more remote areas of the country. These processed food products help to provide rural people with sources of protein.

Transportation

Over 2,000 miles (3,219 km) of main roads and about 8,000 miles (12,875 km) of secondary roads have been built in Senegal. Senegal has been improving its road system by paving main thoroughfares and linking many isolated villages with simple dirt roads. Since most of the materials needed for modern highways are not available in Senegal, builders adapt their methods to local conditions and supplies. Roads surfaced with seashells, sand, or soil mixed with oil and chemical stabilizers are not uncommon.

About 700 miles (1,127 km) of railway connect Dakar with the rest of Senegal. At Thiès the railway branches out to Saint-Louis and to Bamako and Koulikoro in Mali. This line, the Dakar-Niger Railway, connects Dakar on the Atlantic coast to the Niger River in the interior. The railway carried both freight and passenger traffic during colonial days. The railway's purpose was to link the coast—with its well-developed ports—to Koulikoro on the Niger River. At Koulikoro the riverboats coming from as far inland as Timbuktu and Gao in the Sahara could unload their cargo for shipment to coastal markets.

By 1925 the first air mail routes were operating between Dakar and France via Casablanca, Morocco. By the mid-1930s, regular passenger flights linked the colony

Drivers and pedestrians enter Dakar on a **newly built road.**

to Paris. The mail service also flew to South Africa and Brazil. In 1939 Air France began to provide domestic air service to Senegal and other destinations in French West Africa. Dakar-Yoff International Airport is one of western Africa's major air links with the rest of the world.

After gaining their independence, eleven western African countries formed a jointly owned airline called Air Afrique. Each member-country owns 6 percent of the airline, while the balance is owned by a private French airline and by the French government. Air Afrique is a vital link between countries of western and central Africa and connects Dakar with Europe and the United States.

Media and Communication

Two government-run radio stations broadcast from Senegal in French and in the leading languages of the country—Wolof, Malinke, Serer, and Pular. Most of the programs are educational, with a small number devoted to entertainment. An international radio station in Dakar conducts about 85 percent of its programming in French and the rest in English and Portuguese. Radio fills a vital need in reaching all parts of the country, since the spoken word is especially important in a land where most people do not read or write.

Senegal has about twenty daily newspapers, with most having offices in Dakar. These include *Le Soleil* (The Sun), which gives the official government slant on the news, and three other French-language papers, *Le Quotidien* (The Daily), *L'Observateur* (The Observer), and *Sud-Quotidien* (Southern Daily). There are several satellite television channels available, operating alongside RTS, the major state-run television network, which has two channels.

The constitution of Senegal guarantees freedom of the press. Nevertheless, there are laws against criticizing the state and broadcasting "false news." The government of Senegal has cracked down on media outlets that give unfavorable reports. The conflict in Casamance, for example, remains a sore point for the government and the army. When Sud FM, a radio station, interviewed a rebel leader in the region, the government temporarily took the station off the air.

Senegal built a good telephone system after becoming independent. The system linked Dakar with other major cities as well as Europe and the rest of Africa. In the 1980s, microwave relay towers allowed the use of mobile telephones. Since then the cellular network has spread rapidly. It allows people in remote areas and those without landline service in the cities to communicate easily. There are more than three million cell phones in use.

Sonatel, the national phone service, also offers Internet service to its customers. More than seven hundred other service providers, large and small, and about five hundred World Wide Web hosts operate in the country. While few homes have personal computers, many people can access the system at Internet cafés, which charge a small hourly amount to go online. Senegal has more than five hundred thousand regular Internet users, about 5 percent of the population.

MICROFINANCE

Unemployment is high in Senegal, and many workers have to survive on wages of just a few dollars a day. For women, who are expected to stay home and raise children, job training simply does not exist. To better their lives, some are using the new system of microfinance.

Several banks in Senegal offer microfinance loans to people, mostly women, who want to run a small business out of their home. The loans, which amount to one thousand dollars or less, can be used to buy materials and equipment. Some microfinance businesses make clothing. Others make tools, toys, or furniture. By the year 2003, almost 40 percent of the people in Senegal had taken out one of these small loans.

This family works in a tailoring business founded with a microfinance loan.

◉ The Future

Although it has struggled with the legacy of colonialism, Senegal has emerged as one of Africa's stable and more prosperous democracies. The government holds regular elections and has allowed opposition parties to contend for seats in the legislature. Senegal has also enacted important economic reforms and privatized businesses and industries. As a result, the country has attracted a fair amount of foreign investment from the United States, Europe, and Asia. In an attempt to improve its foreign trade, Senegal has also joined a trade union known as the West African Economic and Monetary Union.

Difficult problems remain, including high unemployment in the cities, malnutrition in rural and isolated villages, and a nationwide lack of services and infrastructure. Senegalese agriculture is still recovering from the effects of the long drought of the 1970s and 1980s. Shortages of rice and other imported goods, as well as the high cost of imported fuel, have begun to raise the country's inflation rate. The rate of crime and juvenile delinquency in the cities, especially Dakar, is high. In many urban areas, the health system struggles with high rates of infectious diseases, including malaria, tuberculosis, and HIV/AIDS. Senegal has also been unsuccessful in resolving a violent separatist movement in the Casamance region.

ACACIA AID

The Republic of China is exporting more goods to western Africa and Senegal. But Africa is also exporting something valuable back to China: the Senegal acacia tree. This hardy, scraggly tree helps to fix the soil and stop desertification. China is using the Senegal acacia in drought-stricken areas to help its own environment.

Senegal benefits from the fact that, for the most part, its many ethnic groups have lived peacefully together for many years. Its religious communities also manage to coexist with a minimum of conflict. Senegal forms an important link between predominantly Muslim North Africa and the Christian and animist societies of sub-Saharan Africa. The country has formed close ties with neighbors in western Africa and with foreign countries, including the United States and France. This ability to coexist and cooperate may prove to be a decisive factor in Senegal's future growth and development.

Visit www.vgsbooks.com for links to websites with additional information about Senegal's economy. Find out about Senegalese currency, and get the latest facts on imports and exports.

CA. 200s B.C. People from what becomes Senegal raise stone circles to mark burial sites.

CA. A.D. 1000s The Almoravid dynasty conquers the Ghana Empire.

1444 Portuguese explorers reach the mouth of the Senegal River.

1617 The Dutch found settlements on the island of Gorée.

1645 The town of Ziguinchor is founded by the Portuguese.

1658 The French establish a settlement on an island at the mouth of the Senegal River.

1677 The French capture Gorée and build a naval station on the island.

1840 By decree, the government of France claims Senegal as a French possession and establishes a colonial government in the colony.

1848 The French abolish slavery and make all residents of Senegal French citizens.

1854 General Louis-Léon-César Faidherbe begins the Tirailleurs Sénégalais (Senegalese Riflemen), a volunteer militia, to maintain the peace among rival African kingdoms in western Africa.

1886 Lat Jor, leader of the Wolof realm and an important symbol of resistance to French rule, dies, effectively ending the Wolof rebellion. The French and British agree on the boundary between Senegal and Gambia.

1904 The colony of Mali is created out of eastern and southern Senegal.

1920 The colony of Mauritania is created from a large territory lying north of the Senegal River.

1939 New international flights link Senegal with France through Dakar's airport.

1940 France falls to a German invasion. While Germany directly controls northern France, the French leader of Senegal sides with the Vichy government, which collaborates with the Germans in southern France.

1946 The French Union is created to govern the French colonies in Africa.

1948 Léopold Sédar Senghor forms the Senegalese Democratic Bloc to press for reforms by the French colonial government of Senegal.

1948 The Senegalese Democratic Bloc merges with the Senegalese Socialist Party, with the new party named the Senegalese Progressive Union.

1959 Senegal and French Sudan combine to form the Mali Federation, which declares independence from French rule.

1960 Senegal declares independence from the Mali Federation, and Léopold Sédar Senghor becomes the first president of the Republic of Senegal.

1963 Senegal adopts its constitution, establishing a unicameral (one-house) legislature.

1968 France ends its subsidy to Senegal's peanut farmers.

1970s Senegal and the other nations in the Sahel region suffer a devastating drought.

1980 President Senghor resigns and is succeeded by Prime Minister Abdou Diouf.

1982 The Senegambian Confederation is founded.

1983 Abdou Diouf is elected as the second president of Senegal.

1988 Diouf wins another term as president.

1989 The Senegambian Confederation ends.

1990 A violent rebellion breaks out in the Casamance region.

2000 Abdoulaye Wade wins election as president.

2005 The government of Senegal holds peace talks with the Casamance rebels, but no agreement is reached.

2007 Abdoulaye Wade is elected to a second term as president. By the amended constitution, this term runs five years rather than seven.

2008 For the first time, officials cancel the Dakar Rally, after the al-Qaeda terrorist group threatens to attack the race.

Currency   Fast Facts

COUNTRY NAME Republic of Senegal

AREA 75,955 square miles (196,722 sq. km)

MAIN LANDFORMS Atlantic Ocean coast, Senegal River valley, Sahel

HIGHEST POINT 1,634 feet (498 m), unnamed point near Nepen Diakha

MAJOR RIVERS Senegal, Gambia, Casamance, Saloum, Siné

ANIMALS antelopes, cormorants, crocodiles, hippopotamuses, gazelles, lions, leopards, mambas, monkeys, pelicans, pythons, terns, vipers, vultures, warthogs

CAPITAL Dakar

OTHER MAJOR CITIES Kaolack, Thiès, Saint-Louis, Ziguinchor, Rufisque

OFFICIAL LANGUAGE French

MONETARY UNIT CFA franc

SENEGALESE CURRENCY

Senegal uses the CFA franc as its national unit of currency. CFA stands for Communauté Financière Africaine, a French phrase meaning "African financial community." Senegal and thirteen other African nations use the CFA franc (also known as the sifa), which is divided into 100 centimes. The Bank of West African States issues notes of 10,000, 5,000, 2,000, and 1,000 CFA francs and coins of 500, 200, 100, 50, 25, 10, 5, and 1 francs. The notes carry pictures of Senegalese wildlife and important symbols of culture and economic progress. The 10,000-franc note, for example, shows a sawfish, a traditional symbol of prosperity, as well as emblems of modern communications such as a satellite dish and the Internet's famous sign (@). In writing, the letters *XOF* symbolize the currency.

The flag of Senegal presents three vertical stripes of green, gold, and red, with a five-pointed green star appearing in the middle field. The flag was adopted on August 22, 1960, the day that Senegal officially gained independence from the Mali Federation. The new flag has a tricolored (three-color) design similar to the flag of the federation. Senegal replaced the figure of a person in the middle field with a green star. The color green represents hope and fertility and carries important meaning for Muslims. Gold represents prosperity, while red stands for courage and sacrifice.

The lyrics of the national anthem of Senegal were written in 1960 by the country's first president, the poet, politician, and scholar Léopold Sédar Senghor. Herbert Pepper wrote the music to "Pincez Tous vos Koras, Frappez les Balafons!" (Strum Your Harps, Strike Your Xylophones!). This French music scholar lived in Senegal and also wrote the music for the national anthem of the Central African Republic. Here is the English translation:

Sound, all of you, your Koras, Beat the drums,
The red Lion has roared, The Tamer of the bush
With one leap has rushed forward, Scattering the gloom.
Light on our terrors, Light on our hopes.
Arise, brothers, Africa behold united!

Chorus
Fibers of my green heart.
Shoulder to shoulder, O people of Senegal,
more than brothers to me, arise!
Unite the sea and the springs,
Unite the steppe and the forest!
Hail, mother Africa, Hail, mother Africa!

For a link to a site where you can listen to Senegal's national anthem, "Strum Your Harps, Strike Your Xylophones!" visit www.vgsbooks.com.

Famous People

MARIAMA BÂ (1929–1981) was an author born in Dakar. She described the struggles of women in traditional African family and married life in her book *So Long a Letter*, which won a Noma Award for best fiction by an African author in 1980. Her second novel, *Scarlet Song*, was published just after her death in 1981.

BLAISE DIAGNE (1872–1934) was a politician, legislator, and mayor of Dakar, born on the island of Gorée. In 1914 he was elected as the first member of the French legislature from Senegal. He raised volunteer troops for the French war effort during World War I (1914–1918). In 1931 the French government appointed him the undersecretary of state for the nation's overseas colonies.

FATOU DIOME (b. 1968) is a writer born in Niodior whose best-known work is her first novel *The Belly of the Atlantic*. Her work explores immigrant life in France and the relationship between France and Africa. Fatou Diome lives in Strasbourg, France.

BIRAGO DIOP (1906–1989) was a poet and veterinary doctor born in Dakar. Diop studied in France and joined the circle of Léopold Sédar Senghor. He returned to Senegal after World War II and served as a public veterinary surgeon in Sudan and several western African countries. He opened a clinic in Dakar and also studied the poems and stories performed by traditional Wolof griots. He adapted them into several popular books, including *Les Contes d'Amadou Koumba* (The Tales of Amadou Koumba).

CHEIKH ANTA DIOP (1923–1986) was a historian of ancient Africa born in Diourbel. As a young man, he studied physics in France and translated the works of great scientists, including Albert Einstein, into Wolof. Diop theorized that ancient Egyptian culture originated in sub-Saharan African culture and described his ideas in the book *Negro Nations and Culture*. This and a second book, *The African Origin of Civilization: Myth or Reality*, made him a controversial historian, one whose ideas are still the subject of debate among scholars all over the world.

DESAGANA N'GAGNE DIOP (b. 1982) is a professional basketball player born in Dakar. Diop is 7 feet (2 m) tall and plays center for the New Jersey Nets. In 2001, after graduating from his high school, Oak Hill Academy in Virginia, he was drafted into the National Basketball Association. He played four seasons for the Cleveland Cavaliers and then joined the Dallas Mavericks. Diop has great skill as a defender and shot blocker, but the Mavericks traded him to the New Jersey Nets in February 2008.

YOUSSOU N'DOUR (b. 1959) is a singer and drummer born in Dakar. N'Dour gained worldwide fame as a performer of mbalax music, a blend of African and Caribbean styles. It also takes inspiration from jazz, blues, hip-hop, and the performances of traditional African griots, who belong to a caste of musical storytellers. He formed a band called Etoile de Dakar, which he renamed Super Etoile de Dakar in the 1980s. He has taken this band on many international tours and has also performed with Peter Gabriel, Paul Simon, Sting, and Bruce Springsteen. He won a Grammy Award in 2005 and played the role of the freed slave and author Olaudah Equiano in the 2007 movie *Amazing Grace*, about the abolition of the slave trade by the British Parliament.

OUSMANE SEMBENE (1923–2007) was a film director and producer born in Ziguinchor. He fought for the Free French army during World War II. Afterward, he moved to France, where he became a factory worker and a union organizer. He wrote several novels describing the lives and hardships of workers in France and Africa. He began writing and directing movies during the 1960s, when he became the first sub-Saharan director to release a full-length movie.

LÉOPOLD SÉDAR SENGHOR (1906–2001) was the first president of Senegal. He served from 1960 until 1980. Born in Joal, he left Senegal to study in France, where he became a university professor and a renowned poet. He fought with the French army during World War II and then served as a deputy from western Africa in the French legislature. He was elected as the president of Senegal in September 1960 and served five terms. He also wrote the words to the Senegalese national anthem.

OUMOUL KHARY SOW (b. 1985) is a leading figure in the fight against disease in Africa. Born in Podor, Sow suffered from a serious heart disease at the age of twelve. After an operation in France, she returned to Senegal and began a crusade against malaria. She created the Caravan of Hope, which travels around the country to offer mosquito nets, vaccinations, and medical care to help prevent the disease, which is spread by mosquito bites. Training as a doctor in Canada, she has worked with many national and United Nations leaders in her travels and has helped in the fight against tuberculosis and HIV.

AL-HADJ UMAR TALL (1797–1864) was a Muslim scholar, anticolonial leader, and king of a short-lived dynasty that controlled parts of Senegal, Guinea, and Mali. After a hajj (or pilgrimage) to Mecca, Umar Tall became a caliph (leader) of an important Muslim brotherhood. He formed an army and invaded Mali, later attacking French fortifications and animist states in western Africa. He established the short-lived Toucouleur dynasty. After a siege of Timbuktu failed, he retreated to the fortification of Bandiagara in present-day Mali, where he died in a massive explosion. French forces occupied his capital of Segou (in present-day Mali) in 1890 and overthrew the Toucouleur realm.

DAKAR The capital of Senegal, located on the narrow Cap-Vert peninsula. Dakar is the westernmost city in Africa. The bustling city includes a busy port and hundreds of street markets.

GORÉE A small island near Dakar that was once an important transfer point for captured slaves. A few historical buildings remain on the island. One of them, dating to the eighteenth century, has been turned into a museum, the Maison des Esclaves (House of Slaves).

ÎLE DE CARABANE (CARABANE ISLAND) A deserted French colonial settlement in the lower reaches of the Casamance River. Visitors arrive by pirogue and can wander among abandoned houses, a church, a school, and a cemetery.

LAC ROSE (PINK LAKE) A lake tinted pink from minerals dissolved in its water. The dense water makes it very easy for swimmers to float on the surface. The lake is near the finish line for the annual Paris-Dakar road race.

PARC NATIONAL DE LA LANGUE DE BARBARIE (LANGUE DE BARBARIE [BARBARY TONGUE] NATIONAL PARK) A park at the mouth of Senegal River, covering several islands and a short section of the mainland. Visitors can explore the park in a traditional canoe and, during the winter season, view many species of migrating birds.

PARC NATIONAL DES OISEAUX DU DJOUDJ (DJOUDJ NATIONAL BIRD SANCTUARY) A sanctuary for migrating birds, who arrive by the millions from Europe in the late fall and remain until April. Visitors can view and photograph ducks, pelicans, flamingos, and many other species.

SAINT-LOUIS A colonial town and the first French settlement in Africa, lying at the mouth of the Senegal River and dating to 1659. The town has preserved many historic and important structures, including the Governor's Palace, the Grand Mosque, and the Faidherbe Bridge.

SINÉ SALOUM DELTA A tidal marsh at the outlet of the Saloum and Siné rivers on the Atlantic Ocean coast. Birdlife flourishes in the delta's mangroves and among the deserted beach dunes.

SINÉ SALOUM STONE CIRCLES These stone monuments in central Senegal date as far back as the third century B.C. They mark hundreds of gravesites and nearby burial mounds. Made of laterite rock, the stones stand from 8.2 feet (2.5 m) high and were carved with iron tools.

TOUBA The Mouride brotherhood controls this town in north central Senegal, where a huge Islamic pilgrimage known as the Grand Magal takes place each year. The mosque, which is the burial place of the Mouridiya founder Amadou Bamba, is one of the largest in Africa.

almamate: a realm that Islamic reformers founded in the eighteenth century and that was eventually overcome by the French colonial government

Almoravid: an Islamic movement and army begun by the Berbers in northwestern Africa that defeated the Ghana Empire in Senegal in the eleventh century

animism: a term for traditional African religion, which encompasses a variety of natural spirits and magical locales

baobab: a tree adapted to dry climates, with a thick trunk and small, rootlike branches, that the people of Senegal revere both as a source of food and the abode of spirits

Casamance: the southern region of Senegal, separated from the rest of the country by Gambia

griot: a traveling poet, musician, and singer who recounts stories and histories in public places

Malinke: an ethnic group that inhabits northeastern Senegal

marabouts: traveling preachers and teachers who helped to bring Islam to Senegal and who formed religious brotherhoods that are still a vital part of religious life in the country

mbalax: a popular Senegalese musical style, created in the 1970s and combining African drumming, Cuban salsa, jazz, rock, rhythm and blues, and the singing style of traditional western African griots

medina: the central marketplace of a town or village, where people come to buy food, crafts, and household goods

mosque: an Islamic house of prayer

Negritude: the idea, pioneered by Senegal's first president, Léopold Sédar Senghor, of a particularly African spirit and style in works of art and literature

pirogue: a narrow watercraft, propelled by oar power and made from a hollowed-out tree trunk, useful for river travel or short hops along the seacoast

Pular: a language group of modern Senegal

sabar: an hourglass-shaped drum—along with the *tama*, the most popular drums used by Senegalese musicians

Senegambian Confederation: a state formed in 1982 that included Senegal and Gambia

Takrur: a medieval empire that included part of modern-day Senegal and that contended with the Ghana realm for dominance of the region

Tirailleurs Sénégalais (Senegalese Riflemen): an infantry company of Senegalese soldiers formed by the French colonial administration in the nineteenth century

Wolof: the largest ethnic group in Senegal, present in most regions of the country, and an important language of Senegalese media and literature

yassa: a popular dish of roast chicken prepared in a lemon sauce

Selected Bibliography

Balonze, John, ed. *Street Children in Senegal.* Paris: GYAN France, 2006.
A short illustrated book on the lives and struggles of Senegal's abandoned street kids. Many of them were sent by parents to Islamic schools, which give them schooling but also allow them to fend for themselves on the streets of Dakar and other cities.

Barry, Boubacar. *Senegambia and the Atlantic Slave Trade.* Cambridge: Cambridge University Press, 1997.
A historian from Guinea gives a detailed history of the western African kingdoms and slavery in the Senegal and Gambia river valleys. The author shows how slavery had a deep impact on the colonial history of Senegal and its neighboring nations.

Behrman, Lucy. *Muslim Brotherhoods and Politics in Senegal.* Bloomington, IN: iUniverse, 1999.
The author describes how, beginning in the nineteenth century, closely knit societies of Islamic teachers and followers emerged as a political force in Senegal when it was still a French colony. The brotherhoods remained influential even after Senegal gained independence.

Benson, Peter. *Battling Siki: A Tale of Ring Fixes, Race, and Murder in the 1920s.* Fayetteville: University of Arkansas Press, 2006.
The true story of a famous Senegalese boxer who served with the French colonial forces in World War I and later moved to the United States, where he fought a losing battle with the organized crime figures controlling professional boxing.

Echenberg, Myron. *Colonial Conscripts: The Tirailleurs Sénégalais in French West Africa, 1857–1860.* Portsmouth, NH: Heinemann, 1990.
A history of the Senegalese riflemen who fought with the French in their drive for mastery over their western African colonies.

Lobeck, Katharina. *The Gambia and Senegal.* Footscray, Victoria, AUS.: Lonely Planet, 2006.
This guidebook offers readers advice on navigating and visiting Senegal, as well as a thorough background on the country's history, arts, and culture.

Matthiessen, Peter. *African Silences.* New York: Vintage, 1992.
The author explores western Africa and other regions of the continent and reports on environmental damage and the disappearance of wildlife.

Mbacke, Khadim. *Sufism and Religious Brotherhoods in Senegal.* Princeton, NJ: Markus Wiener Publishers, 2005.
This book describes the acts and teachings of Sufi brotherhoods, to which many Senegalese Muslims belong.

Park, Mungo. *Travels in the Interior of Africa.* Hertfordshire, UK: Wordsworth Editions, 2002.
A firsthand account of an eighteenth-century British doctor, who sets out on a long and dangerous journey from the mouth of the Gambia River to the Niger River.

Ross, Eric. *Culture and Customs of Senegal.* **Westport, CT: Greenwood Press, 2008.**
A guide to the music, art, family life, and customs of rural and urban Senegal, showing how both European and African influences have shaped the country's varied cultural life.

Sallah, Tijan M. *Wolof.* **New York: Rosen, 1996.**
A book on the origins and lifestyle of the Wolof people, including a description of their rural and urban environments, their colonial history, and their traditions, arts, and language.

Sonko-Godwin, Patience. *Ethnic Groups of the Senegambia.* **Banjul, Gambia: Sunrise Publishers, 1986.**
A short book published in Africa about the origins and history of the Wolof, Mandinka, and other ethnic groups of Senegal and Gambia.

Further Reading and Websites

African Studies Center/Senegal Pages
http://www.africa.upenn.edu/Country_Specific/Senegal.html
This university website gives information on a wide range of topics concerning Senegal, including languages, government, arts, and environmental issues.

Beaton, Margaret. *Senegal.* New York: Childrens Press, 1997.
This book describes the geography, history, economy, and culture of Senegal, with useful biographies and a timeline.

Boorman, Charley. *Race to Dakar.* Boston: Little, Brown, 2006.
The author describes his adventures as a motorcyclist taking part in the 2006 Paris-Dakar Rally, a dangerous marathon road race across the Sahara more than 2,000 miles (3,220 km) to the finish line in Senegal.

CIA: The World Factbook/Senegal
https://www.cia.gov/library/publications/the-world-factbook/geos/sg.html
Background information on Senegal's economy, social and health statistics, government, communications, transportation, and armed forces.

Di Piazza, Francesca Davis. *Mali in Pictures.* Minneapolis: Twenty-First Century Books, 2007.
In the past, Mali and Senegal united several times under different governments. This book examines the geography, history, society, culture, and people of Mali.

Gritzner, Janet H., and Charles F. Gritzner. *Senegal.* New York: Chelsea House, 2004.
A book for young researchers describing the geography, history, and culture of Senegal, with maps, color photographs, and useful appendices giving basic facts about the country and its people.

Hudson, Mark. *The Music in My Head.* New York: Viking, 2005.
A comic novel about a British promoter who travels to a fictional town based on Dakar and who explores the vibrant local music scene.

Koslow, Philip. *Senegambia: Land of the Lion.* New York: Chelsea House, 1996.
The author covers the history and culture of a wide area of western Africa, including the modern states of Senegal, Guinea, and Sierra Leone.

Lunn, Joe. *Memoirs of the Maelstrom: A Senegalese Oral History of the First World War.* Portsmouth, NH: Heinemann, 1999.
The author collects oral histories of Senegalese men who fought for the French during World War I. Although the men fought valiantly and risked their lives to support the cause, many Senegalese troops were treated throughout the conflict as second-class colonial subjects.

Miles, Jonathan. *The Wreck of the Medusa: The Most Famous Sea Disaster of the Nineteenth Century.* New York: Grove/Atlantic, 2007.
In this famous shipwreck off the coast of Senegal, a French ship ran aground, stranding 147 people aboard a raft. Only 15 people survived, inspiring a famous painting and a debate over slavery and the country's African colonies.

Moolaade
This film, made in 2004 by Ousmane Sembene, deals with the custom of

female circumcision, which has focused on a wider conflict in Africa between traditional values and the Western idea of gender equality.

Nabwire, Constance, and Bertha Vining Montgomery. *Cooking the West African Way.* **2nd ed. Minneapolis: Lerner Publications Company, 2002.**
This book on western Africa offers regional recipes and provides background on cultures and traditions of the region, including Senegal.

Overton, Cleve, and Jude Andreason. *The Doors of Senegal: Les Portes du Sénégal.* **Washington, DC: Diaspora Voices Press, 2007.**
A guide to the intricately carved doorways of Senegal.

Schafer, Daniel L. *Anna Madgigine Jai Kingsley: African Princess, Florida Slave, Plantation Slaveowner.* **Gainesville: University Press of Florida, 2003.**
The story of a woman from a royal family of Senegal, who was sold as a slave to a merchant. The owner, Zephaniah Kingsley, eventually married her and made her the manager of his Florida plantation.

Sembene, Ousmane. *Xala.* **Chicago: Lawrence Hill Books, 1997.**
This novel by a Senegalese writer explores the conflicts between traditional African society and the foreign European culture imposed by French colonists.

Senegal Tourist Office
http://www.senegal-tourism.com/
This site provides information on interesting sights to see and accommodations in Senegal. It also has a calendar of events and a photo gallery.

vgsbooks.com
http://www.vgsbooks.com
Visit vgsbooks.com, the home page of the Visual Geography Series®. You can get linked to all sorts of useful online information, including geographical, historical, demographic, cultural, and economic websites. The vgsbooks.com site is a great resource for late-breaking news and statistics.

Weidt, Maryann N. *Revolutionary Poet: A Story about Phillis Wheatley.* **Minneapolis: Millbrook Press, 1997.**
This biography tells the story of Senegalese poet Phillis Wheatley's rise from slavery in America to international fame.

Williams Evans, Freddi. *Hush Harbor: Praying in Secret.* **Minneapolis: Carolrhoda Books, 2008.**
In the early nineteenth century, enslaved Africans, some of whom came from Senegal, gather and worship in secret to stay in touch with one another and their culture.

Yancey, Diane. *Tuberculosis.* **Rev. ed. Minneapolis: Twenty-First Century Books, 2008.**
One of the deadliest diseases in modern health care, tuberculosis kills about 2 million people a year. Learn what causes TB, how it spreads, why it is so difficult to treat, and more in this informative volume.

Captions for photos appearing on cover and chapter openers:

Cover: Senegalese girls carry salt gathered from Lac Rose (Pink Lake) in western Senegal. Minerals in the water give it a pink hue during the dry season.

pp. 4–5 The Atlantic Ocean laps at the coast of Cap-Vert near Dakar.

pp. 8–9 Ferries cross the Gambia River near Kédougou.

pp. 20–21 This stone circle, located near the city of Kaolack, is one of more than ninety ancient monuments scattered across Senegal and Gambia.

pp. 36–37 Women and children shop in a market in Dakar.

pp. 46–47 Senegalese women perform a traditional dance to the rhythm of drums played by men.

pp. 56–57 Women sort peanuts, sometimes called ground nuts, at a factory in Senegal.

Photo Acknowledgments
The images in this book are used with the permission of: © Martin Barlow/ Art Directors & TRIP, pp. 4–5, 7, 16, 34, 36–37, 42, 46–47, 50, 61, 62; © XNR Productions, pp. 6, 11; © Roger Tidman/CORBIS, p. 8–9; © Photononstop/ SuperStock, pp. 11, 12, 13; © SEYLLOU/AFP/Getty Images, pp. 15, 51, 55; © Hemis.fr/SuperStock, pp. 19, 40; © Ariadne Van Zandbergen/Lonely Planet Images, pp. 20–21; © Bourget/Alpaca/Andia.fr, p. 22; The Art Archive/Musée de la Marine Paris/Alfredo Dagli Orti, p. 25; © age fotostock/SuperStock, p. 26; © Adoc-photos/Art Resource, NY, p. 28; © Keystone/Hulton Archive/ Getty Images, p. 30; REUTERS/Finbarr O'Reilly, pp. 32, 54; AP Photo/ Laurent Emmanuel, p. 33; © Sylvain Grandadam/The Image Bank/Getty Images, p. 38; © Carol Beckwith/Angela Fisher/Getty Images, p. 41; AP Photo/Schalk van Zuydam, p. 43; REUTERS/Staff Photographer, pp. 45, 56–57; © Jacob Silberberg/Panos Pictures, p. 49 (top); AP Photo/Courtesy of Samba Gadjigo, p. 49 (bottom); © Frank Kroenke/Peter Arnold, Inc., p. 52; © Sheila McKinnon/Mira.com, pp. 56–57; AP Photo/Rebecca Blackwell, p. 59; © Dung Vo Trung/Sygma/CORBIS, p. 60; © Alfredo Caliz/Panos Pictures, p. 64; Audrius Tomonis—www.banknotes.com, p. 68; © Laura Westlund/ Independent Picture Service, p. 69.

Front cover: © Pierre Holtz/epa/CORBIS. Back cover: NASA.